Writing Through
the
Apocalypse

Pandemic Poetry and Prose

WRITING THROUGH THE APOCALYPSE

PANDEMIC POETRY AND PROSE

EDITED BY MARCIA MEIER, MFA

WEEPING WILLOW BOOKS

Writing Through the Apocalypse
©2023 Marcia Meier

Print ISBN 978-1-7329706-8-7

eBook ISBN 978-1-7329706-9-4

Published by

Weeping Willow Books
Santa Fe NM

www.weepingwillowbooks.com
info@weepingwillowbooks.com

Book design by Don Mitchell
Cover and interior photographs (except p. 63)
by Don Mitchell

CONTENTS

Families and Relationships

INTRODUCTION

This has been a labor of love and perseverance through an unprecedented time in our lives.

When the United States ordered shutdowns because of COVID-19 in March 2020, I sent out an invitation to friends and acquaintances on Facebook to meet Saturday mornings on Zoom to "Write Through the Apocalypse." Nearly 200 people responded, and over the past three years an average of 16 people have met every Saturday to write together. Some are longtime attendees, some have come and gone, though all have been a part of our group. They are from all parts of the United States and several other countries. Shout out to our stalwart friends who Zoom in from various time zones.

Last summer I suggested that we develop an anthology of our writings, and was met with enthusiastic yesses. The result is what you hold in your hands. We accepted sixty-three essays and poems from thirty-two contributors, all written about and during the COVID pandemic. Many are responses to the prompts I posted each Saturday; some are free-writes. There were no rules—only that it had to have been written during the pandemic years.

Most have fallen naturally into the three categories that I have designated in this book: Loss and Grief, Families and Relationships, Hope and Joy. A few sing to their own tunes. And that's okay.

This is a deep and heartfelt exploration of the experiences of these writers of the COVID pandemic. I am grateful for their willingness to allow their feelings, beliefs, and experiences to be documented in this anthology. And I am deeply appreciative of their trust and belief in me as editor of their extraordinary work.

Today, in February 2023, the pandemic is beginning to drift into background, though it is still with us. Take care of yourself, get vaccinated, and keep writing.

—Marcia Meier, Editor and Publisher

LOSS
AND
GRIEF

ANDREA VAN DER HOEK

LOSS, LANGUAGE, AND DOGS

I held the once red, now gray-flecked, head of my thirteen-year-old corgi, Molly, in my lap as she died. The vet left the exam room to give my family time alone with Molly's body. Because of the pandemic, only veterinary staff and the families of dead or dying animals were allowed inside the office. There were no sounds but the three of us—me, my husband, Martin, and my daughter, Elsie—crying and sniffling.

When we were ready to say goodbye to Molly's body for the last time, Martin took Elsie out of the room first. I knew when I shifted Molly off of my leg and lowered her to the white tile floor, her body might twitch or sigh. After the fear and confusion of the previous two years of Covid-19, I wanted to spare Elsie experiencing, or me trying to explain, why her dead dog was having postmortem spasms or sounds. I have tried to protect her.

I work as a pediatric emergency nurse, no stranger to death and dying. Most of the deaths I see at work are traumatic, messy, and tragic. I have done CPR on a child, compressing his chest until the repetitive movement of my hands wore through the blue nitrile gloves. I have calculated and administered medication after medication through a needle, screwed into a toddlers' tibia, to try to bring back her heartbeat. I have given breaths to a baby with a bag valve mask, long after the body had turned irreversibly cold and blue, while we waited for a chaplain to arrive and perform a baptism. I have stood by and attempted to comfort parents crying, begging, screaming, for us to save their

13

baby. In the pediatric emergency department, we do these things and then we wash our hands and turn around and greet the next patient with a smile and stickers and bubbles.

I am ashamed that, given what I have seen, and amid these present global crises and catastrophes, I have sunken into fall-on-the-floor, can't-catch-my-breath, won't-leave-the-house mourning over a dog. I thought I was immune to this kind of emotion. Molly went peacefully, at the end of a good long life, surrounded by her family. I have been shocked by the pain and persistence of my misery. The ways the pandemic vernacular has woven itself into my thoughts and writing only serves to magnify my shame—my loss seems trivial compared to our collective Covid trauma.

Yet, Molly saw me through so many variants of grief and fear over the years. She was my only friend when Martin and I moved across the country as newlyweds. When I first saw Molly in the dusty Dairy Queen parking lot in rural Texas, she trotted across and plopped in my lap. She made me feel at home. Throughout Martin's deployment to Iraq, when I wouldn't hear from him for days and was too anxious to sit at home, Molly walked with me up and down along the cow pastures behind our apartment and then watched "Real Housewives" on the couch with me into the wee hours of the morning.

In the isolation of new motherhood, when I reached my limit and considered running away from home, Molly would sit in my lap to keep me from leaving and would give disapproving looks at the screaming baby. Any time I would cry over the years, the stresses of nursing school, the deaths of both of my grandmothers, long days at work, Molly would always stop whatever she was doing and crawl onto my lap, closing the physical distance between us and boosting my resilience.

In the early days of the pandemic, I was told that I had been exposed to Covid-19 at the hospital and was sent home to quarantine. I got through the uncertainty and terror of those first weeks, and then the subsequent months of spread, walking slow laps around the neighborhood with Molly, trying to put distance between myself, my worry, and the virus. When searching for tests tested my patience, I could take comfort in the cheerful curve of Molly's tail, a curve which never flattened. When Zoom fatigue overwhelmed, her evening "zoomies" around the house were reinvigorating. When Molly became ill and we realized there were no treatment options for her, my grief felt unprecedented.

With the amount of suffering that has spread through our communities over the last two years, I am embarrassed that a dog is what made it most real to me. But, when I consider that Molly had been my companion through the toughest times of my adult life, it is no surprise that her death is what broke me; she was essential, my true personal protection. Outbreaks and surges of sorrow continue to catch me off guard in the months since I have last smelled her paws or scratched her belly.

We recently adopted a six-month-old puppy, Greta. My routines have been upended as I walk her miles each day so she will nap long enough for me to get anything done. There is no social distancing from her; she must be within six feet of me at all times so she doesn't chew through (another) Instant Pot cord or take off with someone's mask or shoes. Over the past few days though, she has begun sleeping in our bed, beside me, in Molly's spot. It is not the same, and nothing ever will be. We will all need to calibrate to a new normal. But I am beginning to, after loss, through language, and with dogs.

TANIA PRYPUTNIEWICZ

I TRY TO READ THE NAME OF YOUR PERFUME

I dodge unmasked walkers on the Silver Strand,
rebreathe stale breaths beneath the pajama fabric

of my mask. Toddlers in oncoming strollers
stare. Yesterday, unmasked, I could have smiled

at them. Sunlight slips over the kestrel sculpture
made of spoons in my father's house. Anderson Cooper

shows viewers the divot in the haircut he gave himself.
Cuomo

broadcasts sweating from basement quarantine. We
binge-watch

Joe Exotic, Fleabag, Ozark. The coyotes on the Russian
River

yip by night, prehistoric silver sips. People in Marin

howl now too, I'm told. I pull tarot's Tower card, the
Lovers

next. Chile, Iceland, Denmark, India, San Diego,
Mexico

and Maine: Facebook Live, Snatum Kaur's morning
circle, guitar

in her arms. We chant, we sing from home: 700, 800,
1k the counter

counts, thread of heart emojis like a diver's bubbles on
the screen,

our upraised palms to sky. For Father on a ventilator.
For Auntie

who won't ever see one. For Grandma living with her
two dogs

in Texas. For the pregnant mother in ICU. For the twelve pages

of Boston obituaries. For the ER doctor who took her life. Three
times we hold our breath, once for the self, once for the circle's

every prayer, a third time for time itself, all beings, every heart
beating despite suspended breath. I dream in perpetual zoom,

gallery view. I see you, propped on pillows, your dresser behind you.
I try to read the name of your perfume, the spines of the books

on your shelf, forget to unmute my audio when my turn to speak,
my house shrunk, a wooden star afloat on a sea the red tide churns

bioluminescent blue, a tsunami's curling wave at every sill.
I hold my breath, raise my palms to the ceiling, and sing.

Nina Gaby

Sleepless Woman Tries to Give Herself a Mani-Pedi, Draws Blood and Tears

We are shutting down again. Despite how careful we have tried to be. All summer staying within the bounds of my own little life. Waiting for the numbers to stay flat like magic.

I woke up at 3:48 a.m. after listening to the governor's address and took a long hard look at my cuticles. I balled my fists and recalled a younger version of myself, a person capable of doing my own nails, not what I have become. Ragged and unpolished. Fretful, but consoling myself that in this continued Covid isolation no one will see my hands close up.

I wonder about reopening nail salons even if we don't open anything else. I joke about taking a road trip to Georgia for a mani-pedi. I think about how my own manicurist would chide me, "Tsk tsk, why you not come in before?"

I conduct business now online with people who are in bathrobes or wrapped in sheets picking at the sleep in their eyes, not about to judge my lack of grooming. How many excuses have I made about my nails? About everything? These things plague me at 4 a.m. I can't make much right but, godammit, I can do something about my hands.

I've been nursing a broken nail on my right index finger, toying endlessly with the roughness. I miss my LyLy, my manicurist, who can fix everything. I have waited too long and now we are closing up shop again.

Once, before all this, I was losing my big toe nail during sandal weather and she told me not to worry. I lay back, closed my eyes, and when I opened them again I had perfect red "whore toes"—what a friend calls my summer feet. Another time she eased the flesh of an ingrown toenail with the skill of a stalwart podiatrist. "I doctor!" LyLy crowed, the world righting itself.

I turn on the lights. I can't find nail scissors but I get my kitchen Fiskars to even out the length of my nails. I can get one hand right but the other is harder. Left-handed, I screw it up and try to fix it with an emery board. I give up as the scrip-scrape-scrip-scrape makes my skin crawl. Under a cabinet, where it rolled into the dust, I find an old bottle of OPI "Bubble Bath" polish—not opaque, which would be perfect in a let's-cover-this-all-up sort of way—but a translucent pink. Enough to offer a little shine, but the truth still making its way through. I feel the cool slide of brush on nail, and settle in to wait for the coats to dry.

I am momentarily smooth and satisfied, until I have to consider the fact that, while easier to ignore, my toenails have been catching on the rug and our next season of sandal weather is bound to happen before LyLy can get me on the schedule.

If her salon even survives. *Even survives.* Back it up, I say to myself, before I slide off into the early morning abyss. Swatting at tears, I kick off my socks.

My once signature whore toes need significant tending. Now that I've begun, I can't stop. I bend over but can't reach, and no matter what I do, I can't angle the Fiskars. I end up jamming the point into my nail bed, drawing a single, pearl-sized drop of blood. I try to get to my toes by sitting on the bed but an old yoga injury reminds me that I can't bend that far and I get dizzy from trying. The blood smears my pillowcase. I raise my foot up in "happy baby" pose, trimming the outside of the nail—which drops on my face—but the Fiskars can't reach the inside. Over these months, things have hardened into unshakable mass. I put my socks back on, anything but a happy baby.

I have put many coats over the broken nail of my pointer finger. It feels invincible. Take that! And that! But it's bound to split again and I'll worry its roughness with the finger next to it, unable to stop until it catches on the edge of the world. I don't have LyLy's unshakeable confidence. I miss the hot stones I took for granted as part of my monthly mani-pedi. How smooth they were over my tired calves. How the chatter in the busy salon, in language I didn't understand, would lull me to sleep in the leatherette recliner. I think about LyLy and how little I know about her even though she has been fixing parts of my life for years. I don't even know what language she was speaking. And how, if she doesn't answer her phone if this is ever over, I won't ever know how to find her again.

GEORGE YATCHISIN

AIR CAN HURT YOU TOO

David Byrne portended our doom
decades prior, of course he did,

in that voice trilling and trying
to find its place among animals,

among too much world, too much
world. How handy to have this

protest song for the atmosphere,
this fear of music, this muse

to suggest how to hide with all
the lights on, and perhaps dancing.

And even if you call the background
singers the Sweetbreathes, something

like death always sneaks in, brought
by the call to be near other bodies.

KATHLEEN ROXBY

THE LINGERING STORM OF YESTERDAY

Yesterday's tumult of emotion
Hovers like the after-storm clouds
Still lingering on the horizon
As if the storm is not yet ended,
But only gathering strength
For another surge and flood.

How do you send the dark threat
Beyond the near edge of day
Chase that shadow till it shreds
Into harmless puffs of air
Easily scattered?

I must work on this
Develop the knowledge
And the skills needed
Until a simple wishing
Will blow the trailing storm
And its shadows back to yesterday.

JAMIE WALLACE

POSTCARDS FROM THE PANDEMIC

2020 March 21
The Beginning

I have been riding a wave of adrenaline all week. I am scared and worried and anxious, but I also feel great waves of calm. There is new growth peeking up through last year's leaves in the garden. It's so lovely. It felt like meeting old friends after a long while apart.

The Descent

The weight of what's happening feels like it could drag me down into the heart of this sad and broken planet. We should have known it would be painful getting back into alignment with the world. I wish we'd been more prepared, but how does one prepare for a recalibration of the human race? There have been other pandemics, but we must find our own way. The world is different. We are different. How much we took for granted before we stepped through a twisted looking glass into this new existence where each of us is encased in an invisible twelve-foot bubble. Together but separated. Look, but don't touch.

The Underdogs

Everyone is waiting for a hero, but it turns out we are the hero we are waiting for. This is that moment in the story when we all put our differences aside, and stand as one ... six feet apart. It's the scene in "Ghostbusters 2" when Lady Liberty is animated with the positive vibes of a good song and cheering crowds. It's any movie in which the little guy comes out on top—orphan Annie, Frodo Baggins, Rudy. We may not have the arsenal any sane person would want going into this battle, but we need to make do with what we have. Shit is getting real, and so are we. The physical barriers are up, but the emotional ones are coming down. We're not so afraid anymore of revealing our truth. We have bigger things to worry about.

March 21
An Uninvited Guest

There is an uninvited guest among us
Moving deadly silent from gathering to gathering
Killing with an invisible touch
Making us unwitting accomplices to murder

Our days are interrupted by unbidden thoughts
Of our own mortality—sharp and blunt
Piercing the bubble of our denial

Our best defenses are also invisible
Kindness, compassion, generosity, courage, and calm

March 28
Puppy Love

I miss the dogs. I am sure they don't understand why we are keeping our distance from their tail-wagging advances. I wish I could drop to my knees like I usually do and invite them for snuffles and kisses. I wish I could stroke their furry heads and scratch behind their soft ears, sending love through my fingertips and bubbling up in my laughter.

April 18
Stripped Down

The thing about a pandemic is that it strips life down to the essentials. Time has less meaning and less governance over our days. The bars of our cages have loosened, even as we are forced to stay inside. Surprisingly, amid all the pain and loss, it feels like we have been given an unimaginably valuable gift—the chance to step through a doorway into a new way of being, to recreate the world. It is a huge responsibility, and maybe one we are not prepared for.

The thing about a pandemic is it decimates our expectations of the world. It brings us to our knees so that we might reacquaint ourselves with the earth beneath our feet. It makes us howl up into the night sky with pain and longing so that we might once again see the stars.

We thought we were in control. We took for granted the touch of another human being, the feeling of being in community with others. We squandered our time staring into screens.

The music of the Earth is building. We must add our voices to the tune, and find the harmony.

April 25

How Are You?
I'm fine.
I'm mostly fine.
I have moments of being fine.
No, I'm fine.
I'm okay.
We're all healthy. Knock wood.
We have food.

We have flour.
We have toilet paper.
We have chocolate.
We have Netflix.
I have work.
I'm doing okay.
I'm counting my blessings.
I'm hanging in there.
We're so lucky.
We're surviving.
We're making the best of it.
We're finding small joys.
We're doing okay.
We haven't killed each other yet.
We're making do.
I'm managing.
I'm holding on.
I'm getting out.
I'm fine.
You?

Disguises

Our new reality is putting a lot of stress on the seams
of our personal facades, and things are slipping. As
we let our disguises fall away, we're finding that we're
all looking for the same things: purpose, connection,
truth, certainty, joy, and love. Only a short time ago we
felt so secure. We knew who we were, what to do, and
where we were going. Now all of that has exploded into
unrecognizable shards. The pieces are all still there,
but they are splintered and mixed up. This is, actually,
a priceless opportunity to collect only the pieces that
matter most and rebuild our lives in a way that gives

us what we truly crave, instead of the poor substitutes we've been settling for for so long. My heart aches with the possibility. The transformation requires a leap of faith. It requires believing that we're still capable of creating a different kind of magic in the world.

June 6
Needs

You do not need to have the answers. You do not need to know the way. You only need love enough in your heart and hope enough in your soul to keep taking one step after the other after the other.

You do not need to change everything at once. You only need to commit to dismantling one piece at a time, to finding out where the pain lives and pulling it out into the light so that you might see it more clearly and transform it. Like an alchemist, you only need to change one molecule, pull one thread, offer one kind word, and then watch to see how that one small act shifts the whole Universe.

June 27
Eaten Alive

Life goes by so quickly, devoured second by second. Time's voracious appetite eats us alive in bites so tiny that we hardly feel them until it's too late.

But, maybe we have to be eaten alive to truly live. Perhaps it's all part of the metamorphosis, turning us first into this and then into that, but never destroying us completely. And maybe Time feasting on our bones is a non-negotiable part of the process of being broken down so that we might rise up anew and fill with life.

August 1
To Wander

I am trying to find my way back to an organic authenticity, to being at home in my own skin. I do not want to have to chop my day into little pieces and follow a prescribed path. I want to wander like a child in the forest, following whatever mysteries present themselves—birds and butterflies, fox prints, and faerie rings.

October 3
The Hard Work

What at first felt like a vacation from normal life has become the new normal, and we don't like it.

We started out in awe of the quiet. We watched nature emerge in unexpected places. There were coyotes in LA and birds singing everywhere.

We found joy in the little things, in the simple things, because that was all we had; and we were okay with that, for the short term. But we're not so sure anymore.

In the beginning, we dealt only with the superficial aspects of the experience, not changing anything in our bones. We assumed this would be temporary. But as the months have piled up behind us and loom large ahead of us, we're realizing that the surface changes we've made aren't enough.

Now we must dig deeper, and it will be hard. There will be no more lipstick on the pig. It's time to reimagine our world and our place in it.

This is a time of heroes and heroines, but not the kind with swords and battle axes and hearts of steel. This moment requires a different kind of heroism—one that grows out of deep compassion, humility, and patience. One that strives not for individual achievement, but for the betterment of the entire world. A heroism of healing and stewardship.

I don't know if we are up to the task. My storyteller's heart believes in the arc that bends toward our success. My intellect isn't quite sure how to connect the dots that get us to that happy ending.

2021

March 27
Lipstick & Earrings

I miss lipstick and earrings
I cannot wear either with a mask
The lipstick would smear, and besides
No one would see it
The earrings get tangled
I worry about losing them
Sometimes you have to forgo fashion
For survival
But losing small pieces of you is frightening
Even if the loss is superficial and temporary
Those things are not you, but they are part of your song
And no one likes their song to be silenced
Especially in the dark, where sometimes
Singing to yourself is the only comfort you have

April 10
A Long Year

The uncertainty might be the hardest trial to endure. We are creatures of habit who long for control. An unknown and uncontrollable future is both infuriating and terrifying.

They say it will take years to even assess the trauma, never mind heal from it. They say we don't yet even know in what ways we have been damaged and changed. All our hopes and fears, expectations and assumptions are being boiled down into a sort of primordial soup, separated, and reconstructed. It's like an alchemy experiment gone very, very wrong.

I know that I am different, but I haven't yet had the courage to look closely enough to see exactly what has changed.

May 29
Solitude

I am not ready to reenter the world at large. I have grown fond of my invisible armor, which extends from my body in a forcefield with a six-foot circumference. I am the soft, vulnerable center in the carapace of a transparent exoskeleton that keeps me at arm's length from the rest of the human race.

It seems ungracious—and possibly mad—to be grateful for solitude a year and several months into a pandemic that has kept us forcibly apart, but I *am* grateful. How little I understood the importance of creating and maintaining my own space until now. That realization is a gift, though one paid for dearly over the course of this long, long year.

August 14
Broken

I'm not sure I could handle someone asking me how I really am right now. It feels like a dangerous question. Most days, I feel like an eclectic collection of mismatched parts held together in the semblance of a fully functioning adult with denial, pride, sheer will, and an unwarranted amount of optimism.

It often amazes me that this slap-dash construction is enough to fool most people, but then again most people don't look too closely.

When parts fall off, you just pick them up and stick them back on with glue or tape or staples or chewing gum.

But no matter how clumsy your repair job, how obvious the seams, no one seems to notice. Or maybe they do notice, but they don't want to acknowledge your broken places, because then you might notice theirs.

August 28
Made of Stories

We are made of stories. Stories define us, sustain us, and shape our world. Stories are like stitches, sewing our broken hearts and communities back together—the thread of a tale weaving in and out, pulling us back to ourselves and closer to the people and the world around us. We see the stitched-up scars on someone else and recognize that they carry the same hurt we do. We are more alike than different, story says, just look and you can see it clearly. Where once we might have stared at one another across a void of strangeness, unable to hear or understand what the other was saying, now we have a common frame of reference that connects us. Story promises us that we are not alone.

November 6
This Is a Story

This is a story about second chances.

This is a story about opening your eyes to see the world as it is.

This is a story about being vulnerable.

This is a story about being strong.

This is a story about how things aren't always what they seem.

This is a story about the importance of the more-than-human.

This is a story about how life is short and you've wasted a lot of it.

This is a story about how it's never too late.

This is a story about loneliness.

This is a story about how no one is alone.

This is a story about rescuing each other.

This is a story about finally saying enough is enough.

This is a story about sacrifice.

This is a story about surrender.

This is a story about transformation.

2022

February 19
Spring Hopes Eternally

As winter begins to grumble its way toward its annual farewell, I find that I am looking forward to spring more than I have in past years. I feel like a small animal who has crept from her burrow, ears pricked, whiskers and nose twitching. I am alert and hopeful, my bright eyes scanning the ground for any hint of green. I notice the fuzz thickening on the buds of a cherry tree, and my heart zings with excitement. As the ice melts and the frost comes up out of the ground, I pause to inhale the heady scent of the softening earth, drinking in the aroma of dirt and life and growing things. Water running over the gravel at the side of the road transports me back to childhood afternoons spent sailing tiny leaf boats down the rumbling rivulets that ran through and over the deep ruts in our long, rural driveway. In the springtime, a tiny patch of ground holds an entire world.

The birds, returned from winter sojourns, fill the predawn hour with a raucous and insistent symphony that wakes me not only from my night's slumber, but also from the long, dark sleep of winter. The jubilant audacity of their performance after such a long silence tastes like fireworks on my tongue.

JOAN MAZZA

TO THE WOMAN AT FOOD LION
WITH THE T-SHIRT:
UNMASKED
UNMUZZLED
UNVACCINATED
UNAFRAID

in black print on the back
of your shirt, I have many things
I'd like to say, but pause to wonder
at your statement, all in CAPS

as if you're shouting. I see you're
over sixty-five, surely had shots
that schools required against mumps,
diphtheria, measles, pertussis,

rubella, tetanus, polio. You
never had smallpox, never saw
your children perish from any
of the above. You're free now

to die like a medieval peasant,
except you likely have central
heat, Medicare, and access
to a hospital where exhausted

nurses, doctors, and respiratory
therapists will try to save your life
no matter what you yell at them.
I'm not trying to catch your
attention.

I'm masked, my gaze
on produce as I shop for artichokes

and Bosc pears, available here
in all seasons. I'm looking for

empathy for juvenile rebellion
in the middle of a global plague.
Maybe no one comforted you
when you were a toddler wailing.

CLAIRE VAN BLARICUM

THEN AND NOW

We'd gather for lunch and hug upon meeting.
An elbow bump's our most intimate greeting.
Now lunch is just virtual, all done by Zoom.
We can only pretend to be in the same room.
Some restaurants are open, only outdoors.
What will they do when we get some downpours?
Shopping for groceries, once so routine,
Is now very different while in quarantine.
We do it online, click on pictures of things,
And hope that is really what Instacart brings.
If we do venture out to do shopping ourselves,
The better to check out what is on the shelves,
Then we all wear a mask, and wipe down our cart,
And make sure that we always stay six feet apart.
Unfortunately, there still seem to be those
Who have not figured out they should cover their nose.
At least the TP shortage seems to have eased,
Something about which we all should be pleased.
Feels like we're cooking a lot more from scratch,
And more folks now have their own vegetable patch.
The kids are in school, but through remote learning.
We know for their friends they all must be yearning.
We work from our homes, if our jobs will allow,
But it took some a while to figure out how.
Store clerks and restaurant staff, now more respected,
To be called "essential" they never expected.
Our great healthcare workers are all hanging tough.
We'll never be able to thank them enough.

Many businesses closed, and some may not come back.
We hope that they all soon will be back on track.
Our hair is too long now and showing more gray.
We know to stay healthy it's a small price to pay.
We can't go to movies or concerts or plays
So we find entertainment in alternative ways.
Watching lots of TV felt like wasting our time.
Now we binge watch on Netflix, or Acorn, or Prime.
All the sports on TV now are just not the same.
It's weird to see just empty stands at the game.
We've taken up hobbies, some old and some new.
They all give us something constructive to do.
So we read and we knit and bake sourdough bread,
We'll be smarter, and warmer, and very well fed.
We reach out to friends via Facetime or phone,
Especially those that we know live alone.
We know we'll get through it, The question is when.
I can't wait to party with all of you then!

CATCHING DEATH

"I looked up and saw a horse whose color was pale green. Its rider was named Death, and his companion was the Grave. These two were given authority over one-fourth of the earth, to kill with the sword and famine and disease and wild animals." —The Book of Revelation 6:8

I.

It's 10 p.m. I take my dogs outside for their nightly routine. I call them and they come running out the door into the garage. With Ernie, I simply clip the leash to the metal part of the collar. With Rainy, however, I place both his legs inside of the holes of his purple mesh harness. He has a problem pulling on the leash, and when he does, he makes awful, goose honk choking sounds. Yet he resists getting into the harness, stiffening when he is hooked in. I walk Rainy first and he pulls in different directions, determined to have his way, like if he doesn't, he'll explode.

The wind blows and the scent of lilacs fills the air, but I resist breathing deeply. Earlier in the day, the HVAC repairman came to fix the AC unit near the large bush. He's essential, floating between homes while trying to maintain his distance because he has an infant at home. It's agreed that in lieu of a check, he will take a digital invoice, driving away to the next home on his list. Rainy is lured in by his scent, yanking toward the area he occupied for two hours. I have to pick him up and drag him away, holding my breath as I do so until I reach a "safe" spot of the yard.

II.

In late November when the outbreak in Wuhan began circulating the news, I knew it was a bad idea to watch or listen to anything about it. Unfortunately, I'm drawn to doom-scrolling as much as anyone else on the internet.

You're just staying informed, I rationalized to myself. But I knew that wasn't the real reason. I watched a nurse from an NYC hospital as she spoke to the media about how they didn't have enough equipment to handle the mass influx of patients, both living and dead. One scene showed a truck and dumpster bins outside of the building filled with bodies as makeshift morgues. Yet there were just as many stories of people defying lockdown efforts.

It is both cruel and ironic that the latest worldwide pandemic is a deadly respiratory virus. I have always hated going to hospitals for any reason: check-ups, visiting family members, any occasion where I had to endure the sounds of beeping machines and the smell of sterilized medical tools was torture. It made it hard to breathe as I kept myself from hyperventilating. A step further, I held my breath as a child when my parents drove past cemeteries, hoping it would improve my chances of not "catching death." I once rode in the car with my childhood best friend when she pointed at a cemetery through the window.

"We need to hold our breath until we pass it," she told me. I enthusiastically agreed, relieved that maybe I wasn't a weirdo. When we were able to breathe again, she said: "That's the proper way to respect the dead. You know, because they can't breathe anymore."

Without the validation that I thought I had, I knew something had to change. I trained myself to resist the urge, promising myself each time that death would never float in the air. I would allow myself tiny breaths in when passing cemeteries. When I was old enough to attend funerals, it became easier to practice my own exposure therapy. I had nearly forgotten about my quirks until scenes of ventilators and crowded hospitals invaded my news feed.

III.

When March arrived, I was with my students as they worked on their research project about an illness they were interested in knowing more about, specifically chronic conditions. Most were working diligently, but were also chatting about the virus, if schools were going to close, etc. My last block freshmen found it hard to concentrate because it was not only a Friday, but rumors of school closures made it almost impossible.

I couldn't blame them; I spent my planning period nervously pacing my classroom before walking to the library. Libraries and bookstores have always been the one place, regardless of location, that calmed me. I enjoyed a hotdog and chips with other staff, but not before washing my hands twice: once before opening the bag of chips and once after I gently poured some onto a paper plate.

"You think we'll be out for a while?" someone asked. It could have been any of us since we were all thinking about it. Others chimed in with their guesses: two weeks, a month, the rest of the school year with a return in the fall.

One student coughed without covering his mouth. On a typical day I'd just avoid the area or Lysol the air to make a humorous point. I made eye contact with him and lifted my arm up to demonstrate the "cough-in-the-elbow-for-God's-sake" method of blocking germs. He nodded and promised, "Next time."

For some reason, I didn't bother to erase March 13, 2020, from the board when they left.

IV.

The idea that I could "catch death" came from the spellbook of my mind, the same one that told me to never step on the darker tiles when walking in the mall unless I wanted to die or that if I placed my foot in front of the arrow design on the carpet at home, I would start a house fire. Anything involving disaster or death, I had a method of ensuring it wouldn't happen.

I once packed all of my stuffed animals in garbage bags and insisted to my parents that they needed to come with us during one of our outings. My age was not yet in the double digits, but I was still old enough to understand that I shouldn't need to haul three large garbage bags of stuffed animals in the back of the SUV. My parents didn't press the issue; we needed to get errands done and if the only way to get them done was letting me indulge in my silly behavior, so be it.

I felt relieved, a humble hero. I *knew* if I didn't, the house would be in danger of crumbling apart or catching on fire. And every time we came back home and I saw everything intact, I knew my plan worked.

Though I outgrew my stuffed animal antics, my mind found other ways to torture and terrify me as I got older. My brain enjoyed playing games of Whack-A-Mole with me; one moment I had everything under control, other times there were infinite mind-gophers.

My first panic attack happened at age eleven while experiencing my first week of seventh grade. I was suddenly gasping for breath for an unknown reason. I no longer needed a reason for my anxiety to exist; it came and went as it pleased. I diverted my attention from rituals and compulsions for a time to learning how to stabilize myself during a panic attack.

While faith got me through the early stages of my anxiety disorder, I can say one of the absolute worst things for me to learn as a preteen was the Rapture. The majority of the time, I felt at peace in church and the people who attended Bible study with me. But learning about the Rapture awakened a new set of compulsions and obsessions all to do with what I thought Jesus would want.

If I saw a cross necklace on my vanity upside down, it was fixed *immediately*. I would then say a quick prayer asking for forgiveness. Sometimes I would have to breathe in a certain pattern to dispose of the "Satan-germs" I could have absorbed while looking at something unholy. If I played a track on a CD with the number six more than twice in a row, I had to skip through the tracks until I broke the string of sixes.

I would sometimes see classmates in the hallway with a T-shirt sporting Bad Religion's band logo, a cross marked out behind a red X. I prayed for them immediately. If I saw them in advance, I would hold my breath until I passed them. When I began driving, I never exited the garage without first saying a prayer for safety. If I didn't, maybe God would change his mind if I died in a car crash and send me to Hell for not being thankful enough.

I knew it had to be strange, but when you are a regular at an evangelical church in the South, it's just known as being devout. So I continued to hide my rituals...in the name of God.

V.

In my twenties I was finally diagnosed with Tourette's, a neurological disorder that causes involuntary movements and sounds. I did not know officially until I was twenty-two, the same age I found my old neurology records and saw "OCD traits" scribbled under my then-diagnosis of chronic motor tic disorder and anxiety. Suspected, but not confirmed.

Even so, my rituals and other bizarre behavior never came up at my neurology appointments. Why would I mention anything else that would make me even more "abnormal" than other kids? It was already bad enough that I blinked way too much for a fourth-grader and stretched my neck in strange directions. My doctor wasn't necessarily the best with bedside manner, often talking about me like a subject of a science experiment.

"I observed her in the waiting room exhibiting tics, an exacerbation of her anxiety..." he would say matter-of-factly. This would be the point where I would tune him out. After all, if he had no interest in involving me, I had no interest in investing precious time telling him more of my quirks to dissect and correct. He never knew my need to repeat songs with certain track numbers an even amount of times to "balance" it out. No one did.

And that's how I wanted it.

My therapist concluded that my OCD, even if no one else knew about my behaviors, made sense, all things considered. My body made the rules for me, so to have control over something was the bit of power I lacked.

She also suggested that I should write a "Letter to Death" confronting every little thing that scared and tortured me. I often avoided hard topics because writing them or speaking them meant acknowledging them as reality. My mind sometimes convinced myself that expressing my fears will breathe life into them.

I began and ended at the first few instances I understood how fragile life could be, that humans were not meant to live forever outside of a spiritual context. At age four, my great-grandfather passed away. Around the same time, my family was at the local mall on a night where a bloody fight ensued between a police officer and a suspected robber. I saw the crime scene taped off, copious amounts of blood splattered like a preschooler's sponge art. To top it off, there were two incidents of my family leaving a store right before a fire broke out. Many people noted it as luck, but I only saw it as an omen.

I danced around the subject of the letter I was supposed to write three years prior. I wondered if I should write a will in case I got it and things didn't work out in my favor. That's the ultimate Death Letter, the one where you acknowledge that someone has to handle your stuff after you're gone and it is no longer your stuff. The worst part was this time, it wasn't an overreaction; nurses, teachers, and others deemed as essential workers had to face this reality. Without knowing whether or not I would be required to go back into the building in the fall, I contemplated going through the process. At twenty-four, it was not as likely to kill me, but could still give me disastrous post-Covid symptoms. Or worse, small actions really *could* influence whether someone around me lived or died.

I remembered how much I connected with Stephen King's *IT* the first time I read it. I worked as a marketing intern for a real estate liquidation company specializing in hoarding cases. When I read the intro manual, it noted that many people with hoarding disorder also have OCD. It's all about feeling a sense of control. I listened to the audiobook version as I worked, connected deeply with the kids and their adult counterparts having to face the personification of their fears not once, but twice. Like them, my own worst fears were brought to life, and in order to defeat it, I had to fully embrace the lingering childhood fears to get through the once-in-a-lifetime pandemic nightmare.

Until further notice, the world from the inside of my home would be my involuntary exposure therapy, my personal Pennywise.

VI.

At the beginning of lockdown, I turned to some of the same coping mechanisms I had in middle school: painting and drawing. I have always loved art in all of its forms, but dedicated most of my time to writing. When writing became strictly for venting fears and documenting history, I needed something devoid of paranoia to work on instead.

I tried drawing animals like I did as a girl: bunnies, dogs, and horses, some of my favorite animals. But the horse reminded me of the Horsemen of the Apocalypse. The Pale Horse brought starvation, war, and plagues. I felt the need to resist it, but determined that there was no use in avoiding it. I instead painted it a pale green color. It did not throw me into a loop of ritualistic behavior; quite the contrary, it helped me have a sense of control over our current "plague." I decided to draw it and what it should represent. Nothing else was decided for me. I did not have the power to bring a plague into the world or control how it happened.

Having control over the pen was healthier than trying to control the universe. I focused on the Pale Horse and drew reins across its feral head.

VII.

It's another 10 p.m. and Rainy is predictably picky. He runs circles around me, trying to find the perfect place to do his business. I sigh, wanting to tell him that there is no such thing as the perfect place to poop, but if he could speak, he would probably tell me there is no perfect place to breathe, either. So I let him sniff out the safest place, performing his own nightly ritual.

LISA RIZZO

FLU SHOTS, PORTLAND, OREGON, SEPTEMBER 2020

The clinic parking lot across the street
waits in isolation. All morning I watch
medical workers in scrubs and masks
struggle a canvas awning
onto naked branches of PVC, high fiving
with glove-covered hands.

My windows sealed against
smoke from fires miles away,
invisible, but still tasted.

A car drives in, naked arm juts from the window,
one masked-gloved-scrubdressed
worker jabs a needle — mere seconds
and the deed done.

All morning I watch maple trees crisp
brown in the laden air, forego
their usual autumn parade.
Ash peppers sidewalks, the sky turns
browny-yellow like bananas going bad.

I've been advised to stuff towels against
door jambs, boil water, refrain from
vacuuming that swirls up *particulate* — new word
we add to *pandemic, vector, corona* —
ash on the tongue.

Another car pulls up, arm comes out, shot goes in,
scant hope against what we fear:
the whole world burning.

AMY ELIZABETH DAVIS

CONTAGION

Slowly, I teach myself to let water wash
                stone and change its silhouette.
    But even as I quit assembling
                        watchtower,
            retaining wall,
and dam,
                        I worry that the other shoe
                                will hit the fan

            *

        I worry those long gone
        are threatened by
    a virus then unknown.

            *

Tears come more often.
    Tell me the daughter who left home
    with only fury
                is somewhere on safe ground.

KATHLEEN ROXBY

LEAVING

Leaving the laundry
    For tomorrow
Leaving the broom
    Unused, leaning on the wall
Leaving the bed unmade
    Ready for an afternoon nap
Leaving half-read books
    Here, there, everywhere
Leaving the television or radio
    Playing for company
Leaving memories gathering dust
    On shelves, in drawers
Leaving visions of places unseen
    Never to travel there
Leaving dreams that break sleep
    Dreams that won't let go
Leaving what might have happened
    To the past of almost, but never
Leaving is what we do
    How we live
Leaving this second
    For the next
Leaving this year
    For a new decade
Until we leave it all
    Breath, light, life

Leaving behind for the world
    To sift, and clear away all
Our several leavings...left

TONI BIXBY

THE PLAGUE OF 2020

In January 2020, just like the passengers on the Titanic,
we ignored the signs of our iceberg bearing down.

As a new virus swept China, Italy, even Seattle,
we danced at New Years Eve parties, partied at Mardi
Gras,
skied in the alps or sailed on a cruise ship.

Now in April, we are confined to our homes.

As our ship lists,
I sit on my couch,
next to my husband,
cuddling our dog.

Covid attacks.
The death count climbs.
No cure. Not enough masks.
Not enough ventilators.
Nursing homes ravaged.
Countries shut down.

Even celebrities, like Tom Hanks, are stricken.

My sister works in a hospital,
guards her N-95 mask.
My brother and his husband test positive.
My 89-year-old mother plans to fly from Arizona to
Minnesota
as mid-western snowbirds do every spring.
She's not worried.

Her husband, a retired doctor, told her the Covid is just like the flu.

I wonder, are there any lifeboats?
Will we survive?

TONI BIXBY

THE MYSTERY OF LIZZY ISHAM

In April 1912
Ann Eliza "Lizzy" Isham,
a maiden lady of fifty
and the daughter of a prominent Chicago lawyer,
boarded the Titanic,
traveling from France to New York
for the summer season.

She stayed in her cabin after she boarded the ship.
Secluded and alone,
as her peers partied and danced.
Unaware of their fate.

When the iceberg struck,
did Lizzy refuse to leave her cabin,
sink with the ship?

Did she board a lifeboat
which flipped into the raging ocean?

Or did Lizzy bring her
beloved Great Dane?
Was she ushered into a lifeboat-
—where only women and children were allowed.

When informed there was no room for her dog
did Lizzy abandon her place
to rescue her Great Dane?
perish with her friend?

Because the next day, after all was lost,
a sailor glimpsed a corpse in the roiling ocean,
arms clenched around a large dead dog.

JULIANA LIGHTLE

KINGDOM OF TREES

An essence within the heart of trees
allows them to communicate
with other trees to

—aid each other when disturbed
—send secret signals, warnings to other trees
—express pain, sympathy.

The kingdom of trees now cries
worldwide in pain,
watching each other's murders,
land laid naked, nature destroyed.

KATHRYN WOOD

CORONA

1

June is dead. July and August, too. The mayflies beat their drums into exhaustion; the pope put in his resignation; the world, by which I mean me, which was consummated by one deep breath, is now a land of partial inhales, interrupted exhales, captured screams.

2

Tell me where it went. Tell me where a girl, dressed to please herself, can go be born again as banshee, as batshit, as inferno ?

3

I want to walk into the river and never reappear. Take me, Slick Reflective Horizon. Swallow me.

4

There are a million blackbirds rerouting, changing course—their beaks broken open bleeding at the creases. They convene inside my belly—making haven, blistering home.

5

To them I say: Unsugar me. Pick me up supine. Carry me to a place where I can scream the final scream. These slate colored mason stones slung at God: *where are you* ? and *whereareyouinme* ?

There once was a time I found you under foot, in the boat bodied sky, the holy pillows of a stranger's eyes, but the virgin God is dead: midline split, holy sacrifice.

How can I find you again in famish, in destitution?
How could you ever love a frenetic whore like me?

6

There's a group of people—hipsters, housewives, accountants, witches—gathered at the rivers' edge beneath the globy oaks, watching: "Crucifixion of a Good Girl"

7

It was me—the good girl—and being punctured was a great relief, the epic leveling, the abandonment of logic, to which no one shed a single shapeless tear.

GEORGE YATCHISIN

I WOULD HAVE THOUGHT

that people would have warmed
to wearing masks more easily,
the chance to hide somewhat
in public, to offer only eyes.

Disguised as if for so many holidays
we hold dear, from Carnival to
Halloween, and the occasional
Kubrick sex scene in between.

Nothing is ever hidden as much as
our desire to deny the world of hurt.
So if sickness is invisible we can
ignore it as we breathe it deep,

at least smiling a few more times,
putting the lie to lessons fed
to kids, that sharing is always caring.
How we love to live the no inside know.

JULENE TRIPP WEAVER

SAVING THE WORLD

Daily I sign petitions, give money,
yesterday was so bad I gave $15—
a pressure release—but I did my share,
gave service—now my age is shining through
I barely recognize myself—the teen within sees
pictures I take with surprise—the wrinkles, the skin,
the odd shapes, parts of me falling—
what shows up to another's naked eye?
how burdened life becomes in the push of time.
Aghast, the surprise of age unfolds.
To reason with our demons—what we once gave
with passion—time and service to others—
pinned to a life, a grooved route—
all those days past, I worked to make a difference
in the world, helped others—social work takes its toll,
a battering blow one insult to another,
expected to bend down and we did—
they fell apart in our room and we sat with them
seeking what could help—doing the leg work—
but times we stopped to ask—whose life is this,
who needs to do more? The constant give
with no gratitude, the sad trauma stories
their world thrown over us like a blanket
that riddles us with bed bugs. There is a next step,
a new day and what will we do with it in our aging
body? How to turn to jubilation—or is it too
late—I began the decline from this stream
I stepped into—will I drown?

58

I don't want to whine, they were good years, full
of devotion and love for the work—some thanked me—
but one client called me a cunt to my face
a supervisor stood up for me, fired him
from our agency—another worker walked me home
that evening in case he was waiting outside.
That was one time, there were others,
days I was afraid and walked with second
eyes—you have to keep moving, you learn
to have an undisclosed phone number
to pull in closer, not be so public—not post
so many pictures, one learns to survive
in social work, or it can kill.

JOAN MAZZA

WHAT DID YOU BUY DURING QUARANTINE?

Far from grocery stores, unwilling to risk
going out, I online ordered dried mushrooms,
apricots, and dates, plus twenty pounds
of DeCecco capellini—a case. Plus peanuts,
cashews, pistachios, and macadamia nuts.
Pounds of dried beans, lentils, and barley,
canned beans and fruits. A friend delivered
frozen vegetables, chicken, beef, eggs, butter,
and cottage cheese. I stashed dehydrated
onions, bananas, celery, carrots for just-in-case.

I didn't buy an air fryer or Instant Pot, didn't
land a deal on a cappuccino machine, smart
speaker, or home hair dye kit. I went gray
twenty years ago. I'm hip. I resisted winter
cravings for a weighted or wearable blanket.
Harder to refuse was the call for a puppy,
chickens, and a horse. I didn't even purchase
a smartphone, Fitbit, or stationary bike.
I have weights I'm sure I'll use some day.

Instead I opted for a blood pressure cuff
since I quit my meds. An oximeter, too,
of course, and found new uses for disposable
gloves bought for acrylic paints. I bought spares
to keep new in boxes in the basement: an electric
kettle, microwave, rotary cheese grater, coffeepot.
Essentials! A game camera, too, and face shield,
thousands of origami papers from China, more
bowls and cookbooks, rechargeable batteries.
I acquired and gave away a Spiralizer.

I relented, bought a hand lens to observe lichens
and leaves more closely, then graduated
to a microscope. And I confess, there's that
disco ball with USB cable I had to have at 3 a.m.
after three months locked alone inside, and card
stock I got in bulk, delivered. The sign that says,
BUY NOTHING is obscured by my laptop's screen.
Did you know you can purchase sunglasses
with built-in wireless Bose speakers, perfect
for planting seeds in your survival garden?

Families

and

Relationships

GEORGE YATCHISIN

RE-EVOLUTION

Our friends have the perimeter marked
for a new outdoor bar they hope to build,
similar to the chalk lines about where
the body fell, and that's sort of fitting.

A few yards beyond it we're drinking
anyway, as we've all said double yes
to science, and duly vaccinated can be
together for the first time in a year.

Food and drink as fancy as we can afford,
but it's really most about us just us-ing,
at last in person, eye to unmediated eye.
Historically in my life an awkward hugger,

tonight I melt easily into everyone's arms,
helloing like cake served by Marie Antoinette.

MATTIE COLL

ANOTHER COVID THANKSGIVING

It is the day before Thanksgiving, and I still have no holiday plans. Seventy percent of Virginians are vaccinated, but the number of infections is on the rise among the unvaccinated. Breakthrough cases are on the rise as well. It has been two years and four surges and winter is coming. They say a fifth surge is on the way. If I turn on the news, I see the chaos in Austria and Germany, where there may be another lockdown to contain the virus. And as I said, winter is coming.

In my own life experience, I currently have one friend, Amy, with a breakthrough case and two friends, Nancy and Ellen, who are isolating due to a Covid exposure. Nancy and Ellen were my Thanksgiving plans. I am an only child and instead of a Friendsgiving, I will be exchanging mac and cheese and apples, in Tupperware, at their doorway. It will be a front porch "Happy Thanksgiving" greeting for me. No real personal contact. Masks firmly in place.

Last year was my first pandemic Thanksgiving, and my usual plans of gathering at church friends Bob and Terry's for an "orphans' dinner" filled with people who don't have families, was canceled due to Covid. It was a fun and large gathering in the past, and I was sad to see it go. That year I discovered the National Dog Show on TV. I will watch that again. The various categories of dogs, being paraded in a ring and judged by an official, is fun to watch. Last year the dog show was won by a Russian wolfhound named Clair, who clearly enjoyed the attention of the handlers and applause of the spectators. Clair had a smile on her face as her handler

66

accepted the trophy and trotted the ring triumphantly. I love the dog show because I love dogs, but it feels lonely to be at home.

I remember Thanksgiving when I was a kid. We went to my grandmother's house in the Shenandoah Valley. It was a two-story, hand-built house, with a wraparound front porch. My grandfather Wilbur built it himself and my grandmother Mattie filled it with good food and love. Panda, the black-and-white dog, always came to greet us as we walked across the swinging bridge across the roaring Shenandoah River. Together, with Panda, my mom Ethel, and my dad Joe, we traveled up the red clay pathway to the house. On Thanksgiving the house was filled with aunts, uncles, and cousins, all of us laughing at funny stories about living on our farms and competing for attention. It was loud and lovely. The table was large, and we all fit around it. And after the meal of good Southern country food like fried chicken, mashed potatoes, and pumpkin and apple pie, I fell asleep on the couch across from the springer spaniel print, black-and-white like Panda, on the hallway wall. At the time I thought there was nothing better than this gathering. Nothing.

And now my family numbers have dwindled, starting with Wilbur, Mattie, and Panda. Death has taken all but three of us, me and cousins Jim and Jennifer. Grandfather Wilbur died of Alzheimer's and loneliness in a nursing home, Grandmother Mattie died of pneumonia at a trailer, a few years after her husband, at Uncle Charlie's in Churchville. Panda, the-black-and-white dog, was killed by the mailman in our driveway, while she and Mattie were living with us.

I will talk with the Churchville cousin, Jim, on the phone to check in. He and I like similar TV shows and of course, dogs. Cousin Jennifer will be called for a check in over Christmas. She and her husband, Joe, have Fox news on 24/7, and I will need to narrow our topics to the weather for fear of an awkward moment about impact of the pandemic. It is another Covid Thanksgiving. I dream of the old days, which in some ways were good, and in other ways not good at all. Complicated is a good way to describe my home life. Difficult at best and terrifying at worst. I look forward to better days ahead. I look forward to leaving Covid in the rear view mirror and being able to gather for Friendsgiving's again.

They Really Keep You Going

It is a quintessential April morning. The air smells faintly of lilac and cut grass, silky-sweet, soft, and verdant. The laser-sharp but soothing call of cardinals cascades down from the trees around us, the birds themselves hidden among boughs whose leaves are just emerging, ready for their summer's work. Normally at this time of the morning, I am at school, helping a group of teenagers work on the yearbook, watching the clock as lunchtime approaches and my stomach clenches.

But schools shut down a month ago, so today, after calling students to check on them and sending them digital copies of next week's assignments, I am walking my two eighteen-month-old dogs, collectively known as The Littles. They're a pair of littermates we adopted back in June—back when we could still hug our parents and travel and go to the beach without a second thought about our social responsibility or personal health. Back when things were still normal. Before Covid-19 and its swift sweep around the globe.

I am deep in these thoughts when a neighbor stops his riding lawn mower as we walk by and says to me, "Those two really keep you going, don't they?" He nods toward Soda and Nacho. I look at the two of them, 15 pounds combined. Their dark brown eyes meet mine, joyous, expectant, eager. His words hold more truth than he knows. I have lost count of the times I have told my husband how lonely I would be without them during this experience. Deprived of my routine, my students, my colleagues, and many of my friends and family members, my daily walks with The Littles are one of the few activities that feel normal, their company the only constant companionship I have during any given day. They are my purpose and structure.

My two small dogs have helped me become aware of the small pleasures of social distancing, instead of dwelling on the inconvenience and deprivation. Jarring alarm clock wake-ups have been replaced by slow wake-ups occasioned by snuggles and nuzzling noses. We go outside together and sit in the sun because it's out and we can be, too. They are not confined to the crate; I am not confined to the classroom.

And although small, The Littles have cultivated a big appetite for adventure since I've been home. Unable to while away the hours shopping, going to movies, staying after school for meetings, or running errands, we have found time to explore secluded trails we didn't know existed, often traipsing much longer and farther than I thought their short, little legs might carry them. We have stopped and stared at great egrets, blue herons, water snakes, turtles, deer.

We have also found time for learning. While we work together as they learn basics like "sit," "stay," "down," "come," and "leave it," I learn to slow down. To give myself and others grace. To digest one day at a time instead of flipping through the pages of my planner to August, and realizing every single weekend is booked until then. To be flexible in the uncertainty— because things are pretty backward now. I used to make every effort to keep Nacho and Soda out of their crate; after all, they spent enough time there while we worked during the day. Now, we conduct near-daily "crate practice" to make sure that someday, when I start working somewhere other than the couch again, they will remember that the crate is a safe place, and that I will be home. I manufacture reasons to do this—to leave the house so The Littles can practice being without me. Sometimes I go for a jog or ride my bike, sit in the sun with a book, stroll a route The Littles aren't fond of. They have given me this gift—permission to engage in soul-nurturing activities, time to relish the solitude I rarely had time for before. And when I get home, and crate practice is over, I am so glad it is not an empty house I return to, but one filled with the contagious exuberance and affection and companionship of two tiny dogs with two enormous spirits.

The gentle rumble of my neighbor's idling mower brings me back to the present moment. I stand on the sidewalk. He looks at me expectantly from his seat, probably glad to speak to someone new for the first time in I-don't-know-how-long. It takes me just a second to remember he is waiting for my response. "Those two really keep you going, don't they?" he'd said.

I smile at him. "Yes," I say. I smile at them, the little dogs who make staying home better, and give me reasons to get out. "They do. They really do."

MELISSA FACE

LEAVING THE NEST

"Quick! Come look!" I yelled. My children, Evan and Delaney, joined me at our patio door, where we watched a mama bird deliver food to her babies who had hatched in our cement planter. We sat still and were quiet, completely in awe of her work ethic. She brought food to her babies in an endless sequence of take-offs and landings, and when she wasn't feeding, she was guarding. She stood on our deck railing and chirped a warning to potential predators: "Stay back. Stay away from my babies."

I don't think I've ever seen anyone work as hard as Mama Bird did in those early days of the pandemic.

I felt a closeness to a bird that I had never felt before. My two children were also at home with me, safe in our own nest. We had our groceries delivered and carefully wiped them down before placing them in the cabinets and refrigerator. We worked hard during the day and did homework at night. We straightened and tidied, read and studied. But our efforts didn't compare to Mama Bird's.

Each day that week, we took a break from our other obligations and watched Mama and her babies. If we were quiet enough, we could hear their faint, sporadic tweets. We ate our afternoon snacks and watched Mama fly back and forth, back and forth.

My kids and I didn't leave our nest much during that time. We went on the occasional drive-thru venture to grab a coffee or ice cream. We mostly stayed safe at home, protected from the elements, and the virus. The baby birds stayed safe in our planter.

A few days later, something was different. Mama Bird seemed agitated; she paced back and forth on our deck in front of the planter.

"Mom! Come here!" my son shouted. "One of the babies fell out!"

The three of us sat in front of the patio door, ignored our responsibilities, and watched the commotion. Evan was right: one baby bird had fallen out. It had attempted to fly but had landed on the deck. There was a burst of fuzzy feathers from the planter as his siblings popped out and attempted to spread their wings. Mama Bird paced and watched, offering chirps of encouragement as each baby took flight for the first time. One by one, they flew in different directions and left her nest forever.

We couldn't believe we had witnessed such a beautiful moment in nature. If school had not been virtual, we would not have been at home. If the world hadn't slowed down, we would have missed it. We felt honored and humbled, and for weeks, we told everyone we talked to about our special experience.

I hope to always maintain this new connection to nature, even in our post-pandemic world. I want to always be aware of the beauty surrounding me, to recognize and appreciate it.

Our time in this cozy nest has come to a close. We are back in the world, returning to our routines, and beginning our own, separate flights. I am trying to be as brave as Mama Bird, as my kids and I spread our wings and fly away.

RAIN

I think my favorite memory of rain was just this week. I had to go to an ophthalmology appointment at the hospital and I was scared of the coronavirus. And then, just like that, it rained this morning. Not too much to drown us and make life harsh, but enough to discourage people from going to the hospital, to the parking lots, or doing errands. The streets were all mine, I was calm and they were very professional at the hospital. They disinfected everything, and they were very nice, unlike their usual reception. It was awesome to be out when the others were at their homes, not putting me at risk.

My most beautiful memory of rain is in Iran at the Caspian shore, in the green and colored forests, with a rather warm and temperate climate. We were not cold, my hair was curling under the rain. Mom was happy to be in the arms of my stepfather. She had sun-touched skin, beautiful as always, with her pretty dimples.

I also remember the first rain in Toulouse, when I was a student. I went out into the rain. It was incredible to go there happily without an umbrella. For people there, it was routine, they didn't like it. I was not used to much rain in Iran, I loved the smell of wet dirt—I was marveled by so much free water available to all.

A few drops of rain are coming down right now between sunshine rays. We hear the birds, sometimes a bit of a moped or an ambulance. I wonder, is it taking a coronavirus-stricken person to the La Timone hospital?

JUSTINE SUTTON

ANCESTORS

You brought me here from Albany, New York, where my Dutch ancestors settled and became brickmakers. In August 2001, my NYC-native boyfriend and I spent a week in the city—so much he wanted to show me!—then took the train upstate to see his family. Hearing of my ancestry, his dad took us to Albany and showed me the big domed ovens made of brick that were used to make bricks. The hardy self-reliance of my Dutch ancestors impresses me. I think of my grandfather, generations down the family tree, hand making furniture and designing homes as an architect. And my mother learning from him to be creative and self-reliant in her own right so she could pass some of that hardiness on to me.

You brought me here from Leyden, a small port town in Holland. I'm told these Dutch ancestors, destined to be New World brickmakers, sailed over around the time of the Mayflower. In fall 2001, I spent ten days in Amsterdam with my New Yorker boyfriend. We'd progressed to international travel. My mom was excited I was going to see it, this place of her father's ancestors, so we took a day trip there and I took photos for her whenever I saw the name Leyden on a sign...a bakery, a florist's truck, the entrance to the harbor.

You brought me here from rural Washington state, where my father grew up in the early part of the 20th century. Raised by his divorced mother and Baptist preacher grandfather, my dad had a colorful childhood for sure. He told me he stole a bottle of his grandfather's whiskey once and traded it with the local

Indian tribe for a pony. He also showed me how bears scratch their backs against trees in the forest. He often demonstrated with a doorjamb but did not hold back at all on the bearlike grunts and groans that he knew would send me into fits of giggles as a little girl.

You brought me here from Ireland, where my ancestors were witches and priestesses, sadly persecuted once Christianity took hold. You brought me here from Scotland, England, France, Poland, and places so ancient we cannot know their names. Your customs and traditions and beliefs have shaped me, and I am grateful for the unique blend of genes and spirits that have made me who I am.

You brought me here and I have done my best to proudly carry forward your wisdom, your knowledge. Thank you, ancestors, for being my connection to the universal divine, the deeply personal sacred, the vast unknowable, and the Goddess within myself

JULENE TRIPP WEAVER

WHEN I DIE

*What will die with me when I die, what pathetic or fragile form
will the world lose?* –Jorge Luis Borges

When I die who will carry me forward—
my words, my writings, my history—
in this life I try so hard to be somebody
to lay down a different approach for how to live
amid a world so commercialized,
so overblown with encroachment.

There will be no one no doubt
no one to translate my words
or life into different languages.
No one to amass my body of work,
make sure it is archived, no one
to publish the books in my files
that didn't make it in my lifetime.
No one to carry my words on.

My partner has his own words
his own legacy—he too will likely
have no one to carry him forward.

My friends, busy with their own destiny,
also getting older my sister has no interest,
no clue, and now with multiple myeloma
it is possible she will die before I.
My effort goes with me to the next life
I presume. For I know how hard it is,
how many wonderful people full of words
and worlds have died, people have tried,

but it's such an effort, so hard to even
organize one's own life.

A body outside from another body—
to take on their work is too much—it takes
a committed committee who are being
paid. Like the group that completed
the AIDS Memorial Pathway—such a
worthy project to remember people's lives
and a movement, people who fought a war.
Or Through Positive Eyes, a living testament,
or the Holocaust Museum—why we build
such organizations, create museums.
The Lesbian Herstory Archives, a house
in Manhattan, filled with stories and history.

Certain names and stories will not
be forgotten, but we will forget too many,
the hundred plus names I carry from my work,
my own life that will disappear—
my parents, my uncle, all the pets I ever knew,
gone, as if they never existed. Jilly,
my first cocker spaniel and those after her—
ran over on the busy Route 52, my home
till Dad died, afterward no more dogs.

In my own adult life, no pets reside.
I've seen no cat to their end, only humans.
I was a terrible cat mother—I let go having pets,
said no, and live with a partner who says no,
giving me backbone to be assertive
when I meet eyes with a sensitive creature
who calls my heart. But I am not a mother—
only to my words and my body to its end.

CLAIRE VAN BLARICUM

TO THE WOMAN WHO LUNCHES ALONE

I see you.
Sitting alone at a table on the restaurant's patio.
The server silently whisks away the other, unneeded
place setting.
It is clear that you are on your own,
Not waiting for someone,
Not needing company to enjoy your meal.
Perhaps you are taking a break between the bank, the
dry cleaners and the grocery store.
Or perhaps you are just treating yourself to a lovely
lunch for no reason.
A hundred years ago you would have been unwelcome,
Perhaps even considered scandalous,
Relegated to the least desirable table in the place,
If not refused service completely.
Even thirty years ago you would have been pitied.
"Poor thing. No one with her.
Probably been stood up by her date."
Today, you seem completely at ease
As you ask a question about the daily special.
This is not your first time dining alone.
Confidently, you place your order.
You smile your thanks as the server brings your drink.
Iced tea? Coffee? Or perhaps a glass of white wine.
Even before your food arrives, you dig into your bag
And bring out a paperback book.
You seem to relish the time alone to read.
Your meal comes and you begin to eat.
A clean knife makes an excellent book weight,
Holding the pages open as you enjoy your food.

You take your time, savoring each bite.
Rarely, you indulge in dessert,
But when you do, it is likely to be chocolate.
The server brings your bill
And you hand over your credit card,
Something you could not have had on your own fifty
years ago.
You usually overtip, probably out of guilt.
After all, it would have taken no more effort
For the server to deal with two instead of one.
Yes, I see you as you lunch alone.
I know you, I understand you,
Because sometimes, I am you.

GOLNAZ MONTAGNÉ

SAFE PLACES

I used to be quite a solitary kid and teenager when I came back from school. I would voluntarily go in my room and do my homework; I loved to learn. Being in a lockdown does not carry a negative image in my experience. It is a very secure place for freedom because I have always had a roof over my head and money to live. In fact, life is full of micro and macro moments of solitude, of withdrawal. I feel the same way when I meditate. I like this calm, this lack of noise. I hope to be able to soon hear the birds, because from where I live, I can only hear street and car noises. Sometimes I smell the gasoline because I'm in the center of the city.

Until I turned nineteen, the country where I lived did not allow freedom of speech. I could never openly express a political opinion or criticize the government. I would have risked my life. My parents paid attention to what they said in our presence, because we could have repeated it, and then everyone would have been in jeopardy. It was a form of mental lockdown.

Let's say that I am used to having my freedom taken away on this earth. Also, as a woman, I felt more like a prey in Iran than completely equal to men. Every day I was at risk of being raped on the street or just attacked. We heard stories about the Shah of Iran sending his men looking for young and pretty girls to kidnap them and take them to the king. I paid attention to what I said and what I did. I paid attention to where I went or the paths I took to get somewhere. I think men were a lot freer than we women. So this kind of lockdown, we know it better than them.

The safe places were my mother's bosom, and where I could be with Michel, my husband. He has always known the appropriate and fair thing to do. I was the air-headed one in the couple, and he was the thinking brain. He knew when to save money, when to leave the United States. If we had relied on my thoughts, I would still be thinking.

JAYNE BENJULIAN

PARADISE

The fox had zero
Loyalty to me: human

High-pitched, acid
Scent, not a threat.

He tussled with his siblings
At the woods' edge

Trampled my garlic and mint
Until he came too close—

Go *away!*
I didn't mean it.

I say things in anger.
I counted on the fox

As if he were a pet.
Hedgehogs fast and fat

Squirrels grey and black
Do not dazzle.

Had he been prey
To a fisher or coyote

Or forsaken my orchard
For one that bore more fruit?

Gone more seasons than we shared,
He had his reasons.

Knowing Unknowing

God bless the Ground! I shall walk softly there,
And learn by going where I have to go. —Theodore Roethke

Acknowledge the light. Rest in the heart.
What is your way of discerning knowing and unknowing?

I will remember the pandemic as the stretch of time when I became a mother. In that becoming, I had to learn how to discern what I thought I knew, and what I truly knew—what felt right in the heart, and how I would move forward if I had no other voice to listen to but that.

When the pandemic began in March 2020, I worked from home, cramming a folding desk into the bedroom of a two-room apartment, anchoring my days around a work laptop, and calls with friends—going from computer to computer. In summer 2021, I became a mother. I took a year off of work, and my days shifted, focused around my baby son.

In his early months, instead of meeting other mothers at story time, or in the park, I stayed home. My husband and I tried to keep our son as safe as possible. For me, pregnancy, preparing for labour, and parenting will all be linked with the pandemic—with time at home, long walks as one of the few escapes, seeing faces only from the eyes up, balcony visits with friends on the street below, waiting for test results, and only a few visits from family. I will never know what it would have been like to parent in a time other than one defined by distance and caution. I never had the experience of a mothers' playgroup, or story hour at the library, or the other kinds of interactions that so often characterize early motherhood.

I had always imagined myself as a certain kind of parent—one that would value routine, structure, and teach "resiliency." I wouldn't be too soft, I thought. I would set firm boundaries. After the newborn haze, I delved into schedules for babies, trying to get my son to nap in his crib at set times. I tried to shape our days at home into something resembling order, keeping appointments between the living room and the crib, even if we weren't meeting anyone else. There was constantly a voice in my head, asking if I was doing everything I could to optimize his development. There was always something else to ask, to worry about. There was always the nagging fear that I had failed at some aspect of mothering, in some way.

Alone at home with my son, I soon fell into the rabbit hole of the internet and social media, constantly looking for answers to common parenting problems. Although I had friends I could—and did—call, it so often felt easier to put a parenting question into a search engine. I would then be nudged with ads on social media, answering questions I had posed, and others I hadn't. Was the baby sleeping through the night? Was the baby taking enough naps? Should he be sitting up by x months old? Was I doing everything I needed to to optimize the baby's development?

I treated motherhood as a project to be managed instead of a way of life, a reality of caring and loving. Resting in the heart, and discernment, for me, came with learning to trust my own instincts, and in real connections with other mothers.

Friends I hadn't seen in person for over a year dropped off gifts and loans at our house; offering what they knew what we would need. Mothers stepped in without being asked, and reached out.

Slowly, as my son grew, I gave in, more and more, to what came naturally to me. After months of feeling that I should be getting him to sleep in his crib, I embraced letting him nap on my lap. I came to treasure those cuddle naps, and the time spent rocking him, reading on my own or daydreaming. The days had a rhythm instead of a schedule.

It is easy to think of him being dependent on me, and embracing that. But it was not only that. I found, looking inside my own mother heart, that I was dependent on him. I needed to know I could comfort him. I felt myself to be calmest when I picked him up if he cried; I looked forward to rocking him to sleep and letting him rest on my lap—not only to hold him, but also because it was a chance for me to simply rest. Mothering was full of time that meant getting nothing done but nurturing. This was the surprise of parenting in the pandemic, for me—learning the joy of being present, and letting my son teach me how to be a mother.

PATRICIA SMITH

MY BODY REMAINS A PROBLEM

When I was a kid, my mother dressed me in Navy blue and brown. Red heads, she said, shouldn't wear bright colors. Fat girls shouldn't wear stripes. So I plugged along dully, minimizing my size in solids. Often, I wore outfits designed by Danskin, matching sets of plain-colored bottoms and tops made of stretchy material originally created for dancers. One of my favorites was a set of shorts and a short-sleeved jersey, both the palest pink so they passed my mother's scrutiny.

I'm eight, and I want to play town-league softball. I have no idea that I'm bad at it—not yet anyway. I have a glove for playing catch with my brother, so I might already know that I throw "like a girl" and that such a way of throwing isn't a compliment.

But I want to play.

I show up at the Town Field on the designated day wearing my pink Danskins, glove dangling from my hand, thick red hair kept off my forehead with a barrette. There are so many girls, fiercer looking, all with ponytails pulled through their baseball caps. They look like they were born playing softball, shins and knees bruised from sliding into second base. They throw hard and fast, the balls landing with a resounding thump in gloves. Already I can tell they have a kind of swagger, a body confidence that I lack. Suddenly I know that everything about me is wrong: my clothes, my hair, my size.

Maybe it is at that moment when I begin my obsession with having the right gear. It is an elusive and never-ending quest, this desire for exactly the right stuff, a belief that having it will transform me into exactly the right person. Maybe if I look the part, I'll fool people into thinking I belong. Because at this moment, on this spring Saturday morning in the Town Field, surrounded by other eight-, nine-, and ten-year-old girls, it is clear that I do not.

And maybe it is at this moment that my desire to be an athlete is also born. I want that body confidence and swagger. Eventually, I'll play three sports in high school, all junior varsity: field hockey, basketball, and yes, softball, because after so many years of Town League games—much to my coaches' chagrin, I am the most loyal team member and I never miss a game or practice—I can hit pretty well. But I still cannot throw, and I play right field, mostly with the hopes that no one will send the ball my way.

I love being part of a team.

I love feeling like I belong.

But most days, I also feel like I'm faking it and I don't really belong. When, because I'm a senior, I'm offered the opportunity to play Varsity basketball where I will most likely spend a lot of time on the bench, I choose instead junior varsity again, where I know I will play a lot. I like to play. I tell myself playing beats the glory of being on varsity. But now, late in my adulthood, I regret this decision and the chance to learn from talented athletes, girls who were much stronger and less afraid than I.

And I want to say that now, too, I no longer struggle with body issues, that I am more confident and agonize less.

But that would also be a lie.

My body remains a problem.

Somehow, though, when I am almost forty, I sign up to participate in a three-day, multi-state fundraiser bike ride, the Boston-New York AIDS Ride. We will pedal 100-plus miles on the first day, much of it uphill, and close to 90 on the second, and then a short 50ish into Manhattan on the third. What makes me think I can do this? I own a Trek bicycle, a hybrid, one that isn't exactly the right bike for this kind of distance, but I don't know that. I own a pair of bike shorts, a helmet, and gloves. No other gear: not shoes, no extra tire tubes, no CO_2 cartridges for air, nothing for the rain or cold weather. I own no Garmin or Strava, no heart rate monitor, nothing to gauge the steepness of hills. All I have is my dogged determination, and like that eight-year-old in the Town Field, an odd belief that I can do this because, after all, I love to ride my bike. Didn't I pedal back and forth to my softball games? To the Girl Scout camp where I was hired to teach swimming lessons? Didn't I ride, more recently, with some frequency on the bike path around the Charles River, and for ten-mile treks each summer from our beach cottage to the picturesque town nearby?

I had no idea what I was in for.

Somehow, though, I do it. I train and I train, riding longer and longer, the mileage building. I go out in the rain and deliberately choose hilly streets in order to practice. These are the days before cell phones (at least before the kind of cell phones we can stick in our pockets), and I call friends to leave my route or stop and find pay phones to check in with my family while I'm out riding for hours.

And on a cloudy, muggy day in September, I climb on my bike in Boston, MA, and pedal for three days, sometimes up grueling hills, and then on long flat stretches once we get to New Haven, over bridges and through city streets into Manhattan. Somehow, I don't die along the way, and more importantly, I don't give up—which isn't to say I didn't want to.

Here's the thing: I will do this again and again. I will ride centuries, participate in sprint distance triathlons, ride several multi-day fundraisers including the Pan-Mass Challenge twice, 192 miles in two days, the first one hilly and the second one rolling. I will swim laps for a mile at a time, join friends in post-work bike rides and most weekends, sometimes riding in pace lines, other times chatting as we go along past horse farms, over creeks, through the Virginia countryside riding thirty, forty, fifty miles.

And I will never once think of myself as an athlete.

Still, somehow, I am that chubby girl in her Danskins. Still choosing solids over stripes and bright patterns. Still feeling wrong most of the time. And always, always on the search for exactly the right gear.

JULENE TRIPP WEAVER

A LOVE STORY

Together we age through time
Melding we complete each other's words
the heat of your body warms my cold hands
each night   your heart   our reach
toward each other in quiet ways

On the edge of quiet: music, voice
how laugher and song emerge
two bodies like one, resonate
we rock in separate rockers
I pull   you pull   each

to the other's benefit, we lend a hand
Once we met   we bent our self forward
into each other's life   forty years strong
our pitch and bark   our velvet and satin
hard   yet vulnerable

a warp in the tremble time crosses
this archaeology find: us   an astrological mating
of minds,   my Capricorn ascendant
wanted to excavate your triple Sagittarius
my Mercury head strong   holds your arrow

KATHRYN WOOD

TRUTH IN THE TIME OF CORONA

Symbols are these, I say no more. —Robert Burton, *Anatomy of Melancholy*

Peter Piper picked a plot of newness and scattered it
as dust all across the world—
No malintent, no trumpeting, but death nonetheless.

As we speak respiratory failure parades its way
through the alveoli of the human race,
without pattern or mercy or cause. A ruthless rampant
red.

"It's all very random isn't it? But I didn't want to go
back to work anyways, so—"
The holidays quelled; the bars done closed up shop.

Today, for the first time ever, I sit cross-legged in the
grass outside my apartment building.
A neighbor passing by with a 24 rack of Coronas lifts
one from the box,
pops the cap with a key before handing it to me,
carrying on his way.

I tilt the bottleneck to my lips. It's Easter. A family of
eight follow suit: Mom pushing the stroller
with two of six sextuplets, Dad pulling a plastic wagon
with the remaining four.

"I've had my moments."   "As have I."   Says
everyone to everyone.

The wind too, tucks her head at the fear of breached
proximity, burgeons her love on the inside,

surrenders to the irony of a masked and distanced people masking more.

When will I breathe big again, and brazen?   When will I next be touched without apology?

HOPE
AND
JOY

KM Bellavita

Carry On

We are in the balancing time, balancing grief and trauma with knowing an everyday sort of magic exists. We see the magic in birdsong while experiencing an inexplicable sense of sadness and feel a well of uncried tears. We carry a deep-down heaviness as we revel in the lightness of a day-glo sweet pea flower.

The days of miracles and wonder are our everyday. The secret combination that unlocks them is sometimes as simple as a few deep breaths.

The collective trauma and the individual trauma of living in these human forms is real, no one gets out alive. Even the best tightrope walker sometimes falls. Does anyone get out unscathed? The small nicks acquired while unconsciously bumping into a "something" or "someone," or the giant scars after a major "accident" or "event," do we wear the prosthetic proudly or hidden because of someone else's bad intentions, and do we need the crutches when we inadvertently step on one of life's many hidden landmines? We are damaged goods. This pandemic has damaged us in ways obvious now, ways big and small and in ways yet to be revealed.

We are in a time of balancing, we carry on as best we can.

VALERIE ANNE BURNS

AMBER DAWN

In the orange radiance of early morning,
Heavy headed from dreams and distress,
I sit with green-black tea in hands, sighing.

Through my picture window of longing,
Staring, staring in palpable loneliness.
Massive trees lit with the low sun moving,

Upward to a too-blue sky as the sun is rising
While hummingbirds dart for sweet sustenance,
And a faithful mockingbird is fervently singing.

I beseech nature to deliver days of raining,
Restore faith lost in a chaotic American sadness—
To bring peace to a mind continually racing.

An intricately orchestrated soft morning,
Where the divinity of nature dances,
Unaware of human thoughts darkening.

On the last sip of tea in a day unfolding,
I dream of reprieve and renewed joyfulness,
Another heavy slumber to squelch aching—
To wake once again to amber dawn glowing.

AMANDA SUE CREASEY

WHEN THIS IS OVER

When this is over
I will miss
sleeping until 7:30.
I will miss working

from my couch,
my back deck,
my fire pit.
I will miss
sweatpants and hoodies and Crocs
all day.
I will miss takeout
"because it's just easier."
When this is over
I will
wear a little makeup again.
(Maybe.)
I will go to a restaurant—
and sit down inside,
or maybe on the patio.
I will go shopping,
get a haircut,
get a tattoo
(a heron),
take a road trip,
resume my monthly massages.

But right now
I wonder—
what will we remember,
when this is over?

What will life be like,
when this is over?
What will we have learned,
when this is over?

JOHN GLANVILLE

BEGINNING THE END

Every path has an end,
Every river a delta
From the unknown to the known
Every story tells its tale.

When the time is right
The mystery unfolds
The curtain once raised
Must by play's end fall.

There are times of wonder
Times of pause
The end is not a pause
It is finale.

The author's challenge
To choose a place
Where the end is right
Or at least appropriate.

When the time comes
The epilogue, coda, last note
What will I think
When I begin at the end.

AMANDA SUE CREASEY

2020-2022 (A HAIKU)

Strangeness bleeds into
strangeness until the strangeness
seems sadly normal

ONE THING

It must be fate or luck to be free in this world. A few years ago, I discovered the statistical probability of being a woman who has finished college. I was one out of every 100 people on Earth. Then I thought about other odds, such as living in a Western democracy while I was born somewhere else, having been born from an educated loving mother who made sure we had enough money to pursue our education somewhere else. This allowed us to survive out of Iran when life became unbearable after the religious revolution.

The world was made to be free in, but I wonder whether Paleolithic humans felt that joyful feeling of being free. They had to struggle to find food and avoid predators. At one point, humans were organized in city-states where they independently ruled their area but ordinary people had rarely a voice over their government. The world has always been more free for those who had enough food and shelter to enjoy life and freedom.

Then there was the Greek democracy that led to other equivalent systems that little by little became the norm. There were religions that claimed the right of the ordinary man and woman to have a life. Before the French Revolution and a continuous democratic system, there were many attempts and coups to bring monarchs back to power. If it were not for people who acted when feeling overwhelmed by pressure, there would be no desire to go and occupy the American Indian lands, and start a system of widespread and protected individual power called democracy. There was a price to pay for some losing their freedom, for others to be free on this planet.

SHAUNA POTOCKY

UNTIED

When the heart warms
soft, quiet
when it is gentle, kind
lenient
blind-spot space for faults
or holding them gently

This is my love.
There are pockets of it
grown out of restoration soil
so many years, now sewn
for just a few
good friends, a few
animal companions

The rest is unknown to me.

Unconditional love—
the double fisherman's knot
of generations
that holds
holds

So in these times
alone, isolated
variant again and again
held up in the cold
the dark, the North wind

I tend my rope
keep it supple
protect it
from the tiny frays

that start
the unraveling

Practice the knot
bend over bend
for the day
it does tie in

JOAN MAZZA

I'M NOT GOING BACK

to the houses where I used to live, not asking
the owners if I can see my childhood bedroom,
not driving to Sound Beach to see the lot where
our summer bungalow stood. It's gone.
Long gone are the woods next door where I picked
wild raspberries with my sister. No ticks then,
immune to poison ivy, no foliage off limits, we
were immortal. No fear of Lyme disease or snakes.

I'm not going back to my high school or junior high,
not entering what was PS 98, six stories, bathrooms
in the basement. If I write about the past, don't
assume I want to go back. I'm not going back

to placing personal ads, not mooning over a man,
not chasing after family members who leave me
wondering, not trying to win the unwinnable
or prove myself. I'm not trying to resurrect any

of my previous lives, not going back to life
before the pandemic-shopping out of boredom,
driving 400 miles a week to classes, writing groups,
and restaurant lunches. I'm not. Not making

six-course dinners for eight or ten, not cooking
three days for one meal, plus another day
of my precious few to put away silver, serving
bowls and platters, giant pots, ironing napkins

and embroidered tablecloths. I'm in the post-
vaccination transition, resuming social time, rare

porch visits with friends I love. Take-out delivered.
When I have the urge to get away, I remind myself
I have nothing to escape. I want another shot at lying
in my Yucatan hammock, boxed for forty years, hope
it isn't rotten. I want to read and follow a plot.
And nap.
No screens. No beeps or rings to call me back inside.

To That Voice We Call Fear

We have long been friends, you and I
When I was a child, we met at the pool near the high
diving board,
Which was of course, too high, you were kind to
explain to little me
You tapped me on the shoulder in art class
To remind me I was no Picasso
And that no one, really, would want to read those
scribbles

When I grew up I tried to ignore your calls
And invitations to talk
But in the evenings, you would come knocking at the
door

Sometimes, I tried to talk back to you
But you never listened to me
You always had the last word, and it was loud.
And, so, I decided you must be right.
Though it never sat well.

I was sure you were an ogre, your voice was so loud.
You must be powerful.
I wanted to rip you apart.

So for years I went wandering
Excavated caves of ancestors' memories
Sat on couches babbling
Wrote pages and pages
Trying to see if I could find where you lived, and ask
you to keep away.

Until I finally found you.
Sitting in my own head
The only place you could fit and be safe
You were so small, curled up and cozy, tapping
neurons furiously, like a knitting grandmother,
knowing the well-worn pathways of my brain.
Reminding me of what I couldn't do
It was, after all, your calling.

Oh, I said. You've been here all along.
I picked you up, very gently,
Afraid I might break you in half.
You need me, you said.

For then I knew, you had tried to keep me safe for so
long.
And so I said, thank you. Thank you, thank you.
You can stay.
But now you need to share your home.
Hope is moving in, too.

GOLNAZ MONTAGNÉ

SIMPLE PLEASURE

Since the pandemic, every single little expression and feeling of freedom brings me joy. There is a park next door where I never went to walk. I found it very ordinary and not green enough. But it has something different because for some reason, people have left roosters and hens, who live there, and no one complains about the roosters singing and waking everyone up in the middle of Marseille, the second-largest city in France.

The weather has been so hot that I finally decided to stand up at the time my neighbor wakes me up by making noise, and go out at 6 a.m. to walk in that park. There are very few people at that time, but I managed to talk to the roosters instead, and they come and greet me. I also sit by the little lake and watch the ducks that are fully awake and playing. I even got to talk to the park rangers to ask them to start watering earlier so that I would not get wet under their powerful shower.

I walk up the hill, sit down and watch the mighty cathedral of Marseille far away. I have set up a daily triangular imaginary meeting with my deceased mom and the Virgin Mary on top of that cathedral. We hug and love each other.

Letter to My 15-Year-Old Self

Hey, Sister, no one gets it like me, so really take this message to heart.

I realize that this year for you is rock bottom—you're looking at the scum of the depths. Everything around *is* broken.

And there is this poet who says, "Cracks are how the light gets in." Leonard Cohen. Look him up.

This time is the most fucked up and this is when you are going to start to bully back the bad and begin from nothing, to build a life you cannot even fathom to believe is real.

Trust me, it is better than I can even explain and that you could understand in this moment. But, I am going to give you some glimpses to tempt you on.

You will find your voice *and* you will learn the grace needed so others can hear it. You will adventure and I'm not going to give any of it away for you. You will love and lose—and it will teach you what love really is. It is fleeting. It is a gift we give each other.

You will create and it will bring joy and hope and relevancy to the things others cannot see the way you can. You will learn to forgive, to be open hearted, and lay burdens down—compost for the future. Compost, look that up too.

There will be a handful of amazing people who will befriend you. Take care of them. You are walking your life journey *with* them. Years will pass like breath, gone on an exhale and you won't even notice it happened. Be generous with your time and attention.

About Pat, as quiet and unassuming as he is, he will be your rock of the Earth. I wish I could tell you that sooner so you know, but I didn't get the chance.

Things are rough right now. Tie a knot on your rope and hold on—this will be a practice you literally do someday, and learn how to "look at the rock a different way."

Keep singing, always find moments to dance, wear glitter—make that biodegradable glitter, the regular stuff is proving to be a problem, and go—go rock this life—even the tough times.

For now, in this moment, have a solid cry. Get angry. Break a few things. Keep the shards. You'll want to make art of them someday.

Then look out there, beyond the cityscape. There are beautiful mountains to summit. If you don't know how to begin, go anyway. Harness on, rope up, tie in—just go.

I'll see you in a stretch—and it will be sooner than you think.

Go be wildhearted~

RAINY NIGHT IN WONDERLAND

It's a damp night in Los Angeles. Despite the claims of pop songs and the rest of the country's disbelief, it really does rain in sunny Southern California. The pavement is wet, and car tires softly repeat the news as they roll by.

In my modest hotel room on the second floor, I sit on a small square ottoman by the window and watch like a cat, taking in every little thing. I'm so fascinated, I'm just shy of my chin doing that chittering thing.

Or a Cheshire grin, perhaps?

On an adventure only a hundred miles from my little seaside town, it's an unexpected treat to stay the night in LA before officiating at a memorial the next day. Kind of the client to put me up for the night so I can be fresh for the ceremony, not bedraggled from the road.

If you don't know where you are going, any road can take you there.

Now, my travel pipe and lighter on the windowsill, I'm pensive and dreamy and the street scene below resembles a chalk painting starting to run. In the grand scheme of things, I'm not far from home but I feel like I'm in an exotic foreign country.

Or Wonderland...

It's a quiet side street, not a busy boulevard, and across the way is a restaurant. A small sign says "Japanese Food" but the big letters across the façade are Korean. I am entranced by the colorful reflection on the wet pavement—green and red, then blue and pink—as the neon "Open" sign flashes.

Eat Me... Drink Me!

Moving slowly into frame from the left is a person pushing a shopping cart heaped with perhaps all they own in the world. They and the cart are wrapped in what looks like plastic bags and they stop to examine the contents of a garbage can in front of the restaurant.

Not all who wander are lost.

To the right are two high-rises, lights on in some of the windows creating checkerboard patterns. They appear to be office buildings, but the lights are softer than the standard fluorescents and of varied hues, like a pleasingly multi-colored chess board.

Watch out for the Red Queen!

And in the middle, between the little restaurant that could and the mighty skyscrapers, is a building that looks completely out of place. Painted a sort of terra cotta over plaster, it is wide and low, with a gracious veranda above a set of concrete steps. Sloping down to the sidewalk on either side of the steps is neatly trimmed lawn. The whole thing looks like it's been lifted in with a skyhook and dropped there from a college campus.

And why the sea is boiling hot, and whether pigs have wings?

The rain is now going from a light pitter-pat to a medium but steady rhythm. A small figure in a long black raincoat emerges from the front door of the odd building and turns to lock it before hurrying down the steps, carrying a large satchel and a small box. Bending down, they set the box on the bottom step, then open an umbrella and walk briskly up the street.

Curiouser and curiouser...

I'm at the border of Korea Town and the Wilshire District. Beyond the neon, I can see the spires of an old cathedral. Tall palm trees in the foreground set the scene clearly. It may be urban, but this isn't New York or Chicago. Just a few miles away are the beaches, the canyons, the shopping malls that used to be orange groves. What this place has in common with every other urban center in the world is the shocking proximity of glittering wealth and desperate poverty.

Always room for one more at the Mad Hatter's table!

The plastic-swathed figure continues on with their cart up the sidewalk. They pause at the foot of the concrete steps and bend down, picking up the small box and tucking it away before continuing across the rain-slick street. I wonder where they will sleep tonight as the folks in those high-rises snuggle down in their comfy beds.

I, in Wonderland for one night only, ponder the mysteries and complexities of this world. And the soul we will commemorate the next day, who is now perhaps grappling with an entirely different set of mysteries and complexities.

Why is a raven like a writing-desk?

As I turn off the light and get in bed, making a mental note to leave my dinner leftovers out on the street the next day, I can't help but recall perhaps the best piece of advice Alice was given on her adventures.

Don't let anyone drive you crazy; it's nearby, and the walk is good for you.

JULENE TRIPP WEAVER

BREATHING SPACE

The pandemic gave a two-year breather
like the times I had a break, on unemployment
or going back to school, the strange gaps
in adulthood that arrive a gift from the universe.

How do we go on every day otherwise—a rolling
expectation that can steamroll years, we get up,
go to work, come home—forget to ask deep
questions or hear the little voices inside buried—
forever years, eight and a half in a lab
with its dailyness, its Peyton Place of incestuousness
I tumbled into, so long ago before I escaped,
the little voice kept calling louder and louder
in waves, this is not what you want, there was nothing
wrong with that life, nothing wrong with any life
closing in its web of forever—but our acorn,
our germ rising may be squelched, limited
from its purpose when we continue en route.

I found desire, a wild opening into movement,
the urge to relocate into Manhattan, the big step
I could not not make, like leaving home,
necessary and urgent, to save myself from a life
I could have stayed within. We must talk back—
but first listen. It comes in moments of opening—
a wave of *I want*—a small storm brewing—a faction
of self we hear, curious and afraid, but the question,
like the affairs we make time for out of passion,
how new desire finds a path—opens a door to a
different tomorrow, a new place, a new person you
never realized you could be. We talk back quietly

ask how or who will I be if—or is there a way—
and soon enough it germinates—the seed sprouts
inside, a path is formed and pushed into movement,
going back to school, a drive forward out of a long
deep sail, rich with dreams and hopes for a self
you don't know yet—but who is very familiar.
A song you're composing. A book you need to write.
A drawing from an image you'll never forget, it calls
to you, reminds you there is something layered
underneath—waiting, patient as possible,
for your undivided attention.

DEBORAH ALSTON WROBLEWSKI

I HEARD IT ON THE WIND

"I heard it on the wind last night. It sounded like applause." This is a line from a Joni Mitchell song. I am reminded of it as I listen to the October wind blowing through the giant coastal oaks that act as sentinels outside my own Tudor home. It's one of those days when the light is golden and memories of previous autumns are near.

I played that album, "For the Roses," over and over as a teenage girl, filled with angst, poetry, first love, and heartbreak. My emotions ran raw in those days. I can barely remember the girl I was, with the waist-length dark hair and pretty face, but with a flaw I could never reconcile—a limp. This was not minor imperfection. This acted more like a target, subjecting me to attention I never wanted, questions, taunting and name calling. I learned to walk behind people so as to hopefully go unnoticed.

If you only know me now, you might never guess at the brokenness that lies beneath my polished exterior of the Santa Barbara doctor's wife, mother and grandmother. At age forty-one, I had surgery once again to correct the condition that my childhood surgery could not. This time, miraculously, I learned to walk normally again. Still, the saws and scalpels were not able to cut out the shattered image I had of myself. Any semblance of a wild free spirit was excised with that initial surgery followed by a year in a body cast, a rigid Catholic education, and a marriage to a man who is focused, driven and follows every rule.

Now in the fall of my life, I rebel at my imagined imprisonment. In the golden light of October, in my golden years, I close my eyes and try to picture a life without hospital stays, surgery, ridicule by peers, and restrictions that would keep me emotionally bound and unable to experience the freedom to dance in the wind.

Once again as the seasons of the year change and the seasons of my life change, I crave freedom, freedom of spirit, to feel lifted and light as the autumn leaves in the October wind. I feel an urgency. My winter is approaching.

Should I take a trip to Yasgur's Farm, join a rock 'n' roll band, or experiment with psychedelics? Maybe just a tattoo will do. I hear the wind tonight. It sounds like applause.

Two Roads Diverged

In fifth grade, I recited Robert Frost's poem "The Road Not Taken" in front of twenty or so disinterested and completely bored classmates. I spent hours learning every line, every stanza, so I could stand up in front of the classroom unencumbered with notes while I was reciting it.

Little did I know that for the next forty years, I would be stressing over Robert Frost's words. And, when I say stressing, I mean, STRESSING. Why? Because I thought there were only two paths.

Was I making the right decision to take that job? Was I making the wrong decision to date that guy? Was I making the right decision to move into that house? Was I making the wrong decision to leave my home city? Was I making the right decision to invite the back-up band to my home that night or drive into an unlit campground on a dark and rainy night?

I even stressed over whether I was making the right decision to order a Long Island Iced Tea over a Gin and Tonic at the bar some nights.

If I made the wrong decision, I feared that there would be no turning back.

It took me until my fifties to learn that Mr. Frost's much heralded poem was simply not true.

Two roads diverged in a yellow wood.

Mr. Frost, there are many roads. Where do you get off telling me that there are only two? And, what the heck is a yellow wood anyway? I can conjure up all kinds of things about "wood" but I won't go there because I have to stay on the "right" path.

And sorry I could not travel both . . .

You don't have to be sorry. Didn't anyone ever teach you that it's better to be grateful for the road you're on? And, why would you be sorry when you can back up on the trail and take the other one, and the other one . . . and the other one, if necessary.

And looked down one as far as I could to where it bent in the undergrowth . . .

Well, if you have bear spray and your mountain lion safety on, you can go as far as you want down a path whether or not you can see ahead on it or not. Just ask Bill Bryson, author of *A Walk In the Woods: Rediscovering America*. Do you think he could see all of the way down the Appalachian Trail?

Then took the other as just as fair. . .

Well, there are fair people and fair judges and fairs where the "fair"ess wheels touch the sky, but a fair path? Hmmm, I have to think about that. So you took that path and are justifying it by saying that it was *grassy and wanted wear*. So you're into grass. I get it. A lot of people are.

Oh, I kept the first for another day!

Of course you did. And, you probably kept another trail, and another, and another for another day, including a beach walk.

I doubted if I should ever come back.

Well, then, why the heck did you keep it in the first place if you never wanted to come back?

Two roads diverged in the woods, and I...

Well, Mr. Frost, let me tell you what it took me fifty years to learn. There are never only two roads. There are always more. "Two roads" is a duality that is not real. There are many ways that you can get to the same endpoint. I wish I had never memorized *The Road Not Taken* because it has caused me a lot of grief.

I took the one less traveled by,
And that has made all of the difference.

Okay, okay, poet extraordinaire. Let me tell you, I have taken many roads that have been less traveled by, like the one out in Death Valley that had me bumping along dirt roads wondering whether or not I was going to make it out alive until I hit a ghost town that's not really a ghost town because a couple of people live there. I camped next to Burning Man sculptures and took hot showers under the stars, but that wasn't because I took one road or the other. I could have gotten there many different ways...via many different routes.

One thing I will agree with you upon, esteemed Mr. Frost. It's true. It did make all of the difference.

I learned that taking a new road or path anywhere will introduce you to a world of unexpected places, people and things.

UNKNOWING

Unknowing

Do not fill the airy space
that comes
in the conversation
let it linger there
let it seed itself

Unknowing

Hold back the rooting
to relate—to metaphor
or simile—
instead put soil around
and water

Unknowing

Only let questions
through your lips
ask yourself first
then ask them
to the world
this is light

Unknowing

Listen
listen hard
do not answer
gift the world
with space and questions
now break the seed, root, reach
lean toward blossoming

Unknowing

> When the answers
> are unexpected—
> when hard-heart beating comes
> your gut twisting
> this is fruiting
> this is the life storm
> protect the yet to be discovered

Unknowing

> Turn your ear to the gale
> when the wind settles
> when you can hear again
> the fruit is ripening
> long or short days
> to harvest

Air, aroma thick
with sweetness, with wanting
when the fruit gifts easily
from its bark branch hand—eat it
it will become you
and this will become

Knowing

Befriend the Unknown

That glorious morning on the chaise, a lounging morning without a schedule or task to accomplish. The sink was fixed, the lock now worked and the gate automatically closed. There was time to breathe. The air was cool in the shade and very warm in the direct sun—a duality that provided a background and created an opportunity to make friends with the questions.

Big life questions disrupted sleep. The shifting politics of the country, pending legislation, the recalls, the Oath Keepers flags flying on both corners of the yellow house, arguments over the obvious. Prayer seemed to be the only real answer, praying for this little town, praying for peace to enter fearful hearts. To make friends with these unanswerable questions is the challenge, so one prays, prays for oneself, prays for the upset and disturbed small circle of friends, prays for the bigger world.

The answers will come, come what may. This seemingly inevitable march forward to some resolution, some agreement that contains big unknown answers to the many questions that come. These are the questions one no longer wants to hear, the ones repeated on the endless loop of the times. One accepts that peace comes only when the questions are befriended. Is this the only way to maintain equilibrium in the face of so much turmoil, so much fear, so much unknown?

JULIANA LIGHTLE

I WANT TO WRITE

I want to write about
beauty, wind, flowers,
sleeping in moonlight.

I want to write to
make a difference,
challenge the status quo,
instill a love of wonder,
change the world
even if only for one miniscule moment
in
a tiny corner of the world.

I want to write so that
when I die, they will say,
"She mattered!"

JAYNE BENJULIAN

PERMANENCE
For Karen Chase

Eager for red blaze, Bill and I planted
A Japanese maple next to the house
but snow blocks the size of bricks
Slid down the roof and crippled its boughs;
We planted another farther south.

Its leaves scorched by Verticillium
Wilt, the nursery owner urged us
To consider a crabapple, which inspired
No passion but held promise:
A crabapple would survive disease.

Our two aunts, Sarah and May, arrived,
Wearing masks. Sarah tottered, to steady
Herself, she leaned against the basement door—
Unlatched, it banged open, she pitched
Forward, May lurching to catch her,

Together they tumbled down the stairs.
We could not have foreseen the wind's
Savagery—it sheared off the crabapple's
Canopy, left branches dangling
At the elbows, the crown on its side in the dirt.

It might grow roots, Let's replant it—
Bill, recalling how he had staked
An avocado on toothpicks in glass.
I thought we could prune the branches,
Coax them outward, concession

To diminished hope. Sarah and May
Broke many bones, but survived.
We had no plan. We planted.

The Gift to be a Writer

The thing about writing is you have to keep
reassuring yourself, to look inside and take
time to go to the page, to open to vulnerability
to share even in the face of rejection.

The thing about writing is it has no end
like you have no end, your trails are many
to follow—start with your name—your interest,
your obsessions—open your barrels of shame
take out the laundry onto the page—and read.

We are truly endless, one line can take
me to a multitude of what seems impossible
to express—and we keep writing.
We must counterbalance the desire to stop—
not put down what simmers beneath the daily
swell of endless tasks to stay alive and functioning.
We work best when fully invested in sorting-out
what lies inside. Even and especially when afraid.

Take classes, sit in groups. Open painful memories
and joyous ones. As much as finding love it is a drive.
As much as giving birth it is a rise—to be a person
who documents, who takes the time to pull moments
into words. Some say they want to write
but time doesn't form to make it happen.

We are a scaffold of bright lights burning through time
electrical beings interconnected. Why we gather, why we
are drawn to some and not to others and that magic
when we connect. And on the page, we form our self
anew each time—discover our inside self, how it differs

from outside self. The memories, our personal history
how it interacts with the events of the world.

How we figure out what is right for us—the multiplicity
of ways to move forward despite, and using feedback
even when rejected, taking it not as obliteration—
but as a force to boomerang back our words—
sometimes with edits—sometimes without.
We are our words, we ourselves a force beyond
words, indescribable and that is why we must
keep defining this impossible task.

Within this time defining lies endless possibility,
endless capacity nuanced through our words,
our one and only lifetime to live, to express
on the page, this the gift to be a writer.

AMANDA SUE CREASEY

AIRBORNE

An osprey catches
an updraft,
hovers above the highway bridge—
balanced between blue river, blue sky.

When I arrive
on my parents' porch,
they do not come out.
I do not go in.
We do not hug.

We talk through the screen door, their faces
dim. I fight
the urge to lean in closer.

When I leave, some of their fear
follows me, heavy, weighted. And I think
of the osprey—
high above it all, unaware, unaffected, free.

LISA RIZZO

PRACTICE IN PANDEMIC

In a house filled with Zoom workers,
       I try to hold the lotus in my mind but
             the coffee pot just bubbled
     I hear John's voice talking
       about some IT gobbledygook
         and outside someone is weed
whacking again

I cup my hands, hope to receive peace
     until I remember
     Lawrence Ferlinghetti died yesterday
       I read one of his poems
   in high school
     English class and of course it was about
Jesus on the cross
    which back then
      I still believed in
        but today when I Googled it
          found it was more about
social justice
    before anyone called it that
      and I wonder what my young girl-self
thought
    it was the '70s after all
      and that young girl so earnest
        but didn't yet know she could
write a poem so

I breathe in and out, try to still my heart until

the coffee's sweet and bitter aroma
(how can it be both bitter and sweet?)
brings me back to Rome—years ago—

sun setting over the Tiber,
a stone bridge rough and age-pitted
I lean over the river
listen to Italian flowing
light burnishing
domes into pink lotus buds
as bells ring out
all is well
va bene va bene

PATRICIA SMITH

REIMAGINING SCHOOLS

For the past several weeks, on leave from teaching while I recover from hip surgery, I have been sitting propped on pillows and packed with ice thinking and reading about all the criticisms of schools: closings and mask mandates and fearful teachers. In one article, the writer chastises schools for not allowing kids the pleasures of growing up, as if not having Homecoming dance will ruin their young lives, or that trying to keep them physically distanced is akin to forcing social isolation.

I will tell you–I hate teaching in a mask. There are physical inconveniences: I get hot, my glasses are perpetually foggy, physical exertion is more difficult (how *do* those nurses do it?). I drink less water than I should. And then there are the communication problems: it's harder to understand the kids when they're wearing masks, and they struggle to understand us, too.

And yet–I'm happy to comply, happy that my students comply. We put up with far worse–for instance, active shooter drills. Where are all the op eds and essays and angry Facebook posts about that? Aren't active shooter drills–those awful minutes spent in dark, eerie silence, huddled and hidden behind locked doors, someone outside the classroom acting the part, jangling the doorknob and all our nerves, each of us imagining what it would be *really like*–damaging to our mental health?

We want to say to the students: It won't ever happen *here*, but as families at Columbine, Sandy Hook, Marjory Stoneman Douglas and far, far too many other schools know all too well, it *could*. So we tell our students: It's best to be prepared. It would be reckless not to.

Now here we are, in the midst of a pandemic, where trying to prevent the worst might mean canceling the pep rally or God forbid, the prom. It might mean curtailing sports. Or wearing masks. Wouldn't it be reckless not to?

I wish instead of lamenting the loss of whatever their writers feel nostalgic for, that the essays and op eds demanded a new way to do school. I could buy into that. Why aren't we insisting on the end of standardized testing? Why, instead of taking schools and by extension, those of us who work in them, to task, aren't we asking ourselves, *how did we let things get this way?* How is it okay that school is sometimes a kid's only safe haven? The only place they can get a meal? Why have many of us accepted that school shooter drills and metal detectors and police on staff are a given? We are asking schools and teachers to do nearly impossible work, and in general, paying us very little to do it.

I don't think any of us become teachers for the salary, but it would be nice, for example, if we could afford to live in the towns where we teach. Or when we're required to take classes for certification or want to improve our content knowledge or teaching skills, there's money available. It would be nice if when we needed books for our classrooms, we could buy them and didn't have to rely on GoFundMe or Donors Choose. Let's not even talk about school building repairs, or in these pandemic-days, a working ventilation system.

We say we value children and families, but when, in a pandemic, our societal shortcomings become glaringly obvious—the lack of affordable child care or paid time off for parents, or rent subsidies or a livable minimum wage—suddenly everything becomes the fault of schools. Suddenly closing schools becomes the No. 1 reason behind the mental health crisis facing our kids.

In-person learning *is* best, I agree. But isn't it also ironic that while many parents clamor for in-person school, many of those same parents want greater control over what their kids are being taught? Some parents seem to suggest that they know more about educating their kids than the very schools they are wanting to keep open and the professional educators who teach in them. In-person learning is best, they say, but be sure you don't talk about race or racism. Don't read books like Toni Morrison's Pulitzer-Prize winning book *Beloved.* Don't teach anything meaningful about American history. Don't do anything to make schools a safe haven for queer or trans kids, either. But let's make sure we say the Pledge of Allegiance. Enforce outdated dress codes. Let's make sure we keep schools exactly like they have been forever in terms of course content and classroom design.

Of course, all schools aren't like this, even all public schools. As an alumni interviewer for Wesleyan University, I have been awed by many passionate young people who have thrived and are thriving, in spite of virtual learning and continued COVID restrictions. I have heard of incredible innovations, fascinating coursework, devoted teachers in all kinds of schools—large and urban, small and suburban, public and private. And my own students continue to inspire me, too. Even on Zoom last year, they participated in intellectually vibrant discussions and supportive, creative classroom communities. It wasn't *all* a wash.

So I guess what I'm asking for is a word I've heard tossed around a lot these days—grace. Instead of demanding that schools go back to "normal," can we first acknowledge that in some cases, normal isn't ideal anyway? Instead, can we try to focus on what matters the most? Can we start to consider that for the foreseeable future there just might be moments of necessary online learning? Can we take the time to plan for this ongoing pandemic?

And maybe what I'm also asking is for us to collectively pose the question:

What is the purpose of school? And what is the job of a teacher? I might tell you it's holy work (but that's an entirely different essay), so instead I'll say this: for thirty-six years, my job as a teacher has been to help students figure out who they are, to help them become their true selves. These days, I happen to do that by teaching high school juniors to look closely at literature, to consider deeply what they read, to figure out what they think and why; to learn how to express in writing those opinions and thoughts. And I teach writers of all ages to tell the stories most important to them.

If we want to reimagine what school can look like, I'm in and eager for the discussion. The blame game has gone on long enough. Let's fire up our imaginations instead and see what might emerge. Let's bring our best collaborative spirits to the table. How might we re-imagine our communities? And our schools?

TIME PASSAGE

The warm September sun reached the edge of the horizon, painting the stone buildings of Sudjuradj village the soft color of honey. Returning to this small island Šipan in Croatia, where I've spent endless summers of my youth, simultaneously filled me with excitement and dread.

I stood on the starboard side of the ferry, anxiously scanning the shore, searching for my parents. As we neared the landing, the diesel engine of the ferry groaned louder.

Pandemic insinuated itself into our lives, delaying my visit by two years, which, for my ninety years old parents, represents an eternity. While my parents live in Slovenia, they spend their time from May through October on this jewel of an island in the neighboring country of Croatia. They built a small summer cottage when my brother and I were still snotty brats kicking soccer ball in the village square with local kids. I live in California, and with the entire world in lockdown, I haven't been able to be with my parents when they needed me most. The isolation and the fear of the unknown plunged my mother into a debilitating depression. My father, always my anchor, has been diagnosed with dementia since my last visit. For the first time in many years, they haven't been able to migrate to the island for the summer, uncertain if they would ever be able to return.

Finally, things relaxed in the spring of 2021. As soon as my parents received the COVID-19 vaccinations and a blessing from their doctor, my brother packed up the car and drove them to their island.

International travel was still on hold. Time crawled. Finally, I received my second COVID vaccination and the green light to book my flight. I was going home to see my parents at last.

When I arrived at Reno, Nevada, airport, the line stretched to infinity and beyond. Reaching the counter with no time to spare, I handed my negative COVID-19 test results and my passport to a stern-looking agent at the airline counter. She informed me I needed additional health documents: one to pass through London, England, the other to fly to Vienna, Austria.

"Do you have the forms?" I asked. "You need to download an app and fill them out online," she answered briskly, and turned to the next passenger.

That set the tone for the next twenty-four hours of missed flights, endless lines, and anxious looking eyes peering above the face masks into the confines of the crowded airplane. The world was ready to travel again; I just wanted to fly home. When I finally landed at Vienna airport more than twelve hours after I was supposed to, I learned that my luggage was lost in the bowels of Heathrow Airport and would stay there for the reminder of my trip. On a five-hour train ride from Vienna to Bled station in Slovenia, mountains, trees, churches, and cows streamed by until I couldn't keep my eyes open any longer. I was awakened by a toot of the train whistle announcing the arrival at a station a mile away from my childhood home. My journey wasn't over yet.

"Aren't you going to stay to rest?" my brother pleaded with me when he picked me up. "I have to go see them,"

I said. He understood and handed me the keys to his car. At home I quickly showered and took off on a ten-hour drive toward the ancient fortress city of Dubrovnik. Stopping only once for gas and a pee break, I caught the island ferry at the port of Dubrovnik in the nick of time.

For the next hour, I stood on the upper deck, holding tight onto the railing until we rounded the lighthouse point and entered the bay. I imagined my parents hurrying down the many steps to meet me. In my mind's eye, I could see my father pacing back and forth on the old marble-stone dock, his hands folded behind his back, which now bends like the bow of an old fishing boat.

But something was wrong. I couldn't see my parents. The expectation caused my heart to thump in my tightening throat, and droplets of cold sweat like tiny pearls collected on my upper lip. What if my father fell on the steep stairs leading toward the harbor? Perhaps my mother suffered another nervous breakdown? Maybe Father had another stroke? I am too late, too late, too late... The words reverberated through my entire body like the rumbling of the ferry's old diesel engine. My parents always wait for the ship, even if they are not expecting anyone.

Where were they?

I felt acid rising in my throat and wanted to jump off the ferry before it was even docked. The turbine engine revved and lurched into reverse and the captain expertly aligned the stern of the ferry with the shore. The deckhand threw the thick line to the outstretched arms of a man on the dock, who looped it to the cast iron bollard. I grabbed my handbag and ran, dodging passengers disembarking ahead of me.

I ran through the village across the ancient marble stones. The sea was to my right. Blue-and-white-painted fishing boats were tied up, rust-colored fishing nets piled in their bows.

The narrow stone path led me up the hill. Bougainvillea branches thick with magenta blossoms hung off the walls on both sides of the path. I took the right turn onto an even smaller and narrower trail winding among the olive trees— and stopped.

Before me stood a small white marble stone house with a red terracotta roof. The green shutters of the two tiny windows on the east side of the house were closed. It appeared as if no one lived there anymore. I let go of the handle of my bag and wrapped my arms around my trembling body.

The house used to look so much bigger when I was a child. There were several olive trees surrounding it. Some of the larger branches hung over the roof, threatening to swallow it up. They needed to be cut. The grape vine, loaded with dark purple grapes that drooped off it like oversized jewels, was shading the terrace. Waist high purple flowers lined the remaining part of the path leading up to our tiny cottage. Sweet scent of lavender permeated the air and my body vibrated with the shrill of the cicada's mating song.

Mother rounded the corner, carrying a green watering can. Startled, she looked up at me, pressed her left hand tightly against her mouth and dropped the can. The water spilled onto the stone path and disappeared through the cracks. I held my breath and waited for her words to come.

"Oh, Jesus, Marija!" Mother's call for help penetrated the silence and my father, all bent over, came shuffling from the terrace. He looked frightened, like a little bird. They both stood there, holding hands, staring at me as if I were an apparition.

Then Father turned to Mother and asked, "Who is this?" My breath left me when he added, "What is she doing here?" His raspy voice filled the air like shattered glass.

My legs were wobbly. I lowered myself slowly onto the stone wall behind me. Mother gently touched his arm, "Your daughter," she whispered into his ear. He stepped back, looking confused. The air was thick with pain. My throat tightened even more. I was desperately trying to hide my shock at seeing both of my parents so frail.

"We weren't expecting you until tomorrow!" The tears welled up in the corners of Mother's eyes and she looked so vulnerable, fragile, feeling sorry she mixed up the days of my arrival, but at that moment, as I sat on the ancient wall, trying to find my breath and my words, no one was sorrier than I. Sorry for all the years of my absence, sorry for the lost time never to be regained.

I rose, made a step in their direction to erase the distance, erase the years since we last hugged. Slowly, I walked toward my father, afraid that if I moved too fast, he would topple backward or fly away. I stood before him and he, bent over like a weeping willow, leaned over to stroke my cheek. His milky blue eyes stared into mine for infinite moments. His bony fingers trailed down my cheek, then paused at my lips, as if a blind man was reading my face by Braille. Finally, my father whispered my name, and it floated in my direction on the soft evening breeze rising from the sea.

In the morning, the rumble of the ferry's diesel engine woke up the village. We sat on the terrace, just the three of us, drinking coffee, and together we watched the sun rising out of the Adriatic ocean. Not all was lost, not yet. I was home.

AMY ELIZABETH DAVIS

QUARANTINE MIND

Instead of leaving home,
    we play the blues from disks of shellac
you found in your grandparents' attic.
    I sit by an open window,
      looking for the aroma of dropping evening,
  drifting in a truncated
spectrum. Blue fire. Blue ice.
    Blue crab and Blue corn.

           Wrapped in an ancient quilt
of cotton bits worn shiny, I wander in the bits of day
      that sometimes enter
          sleep. But I am awake,
  though as disoriented
as after the rapid
shifts
          of dreams.
Without
moving, I find myself
in new settings,

  climbing steep flagstone
    steps made slippery by ice,
crossing a meadow under
  a cool summer sky,
absorbing the nighttime smell
of its tall grasses. I pull the bedspread
tight against the breeze.

          *

The patchwork envisioned by the quarantine mind
        has nothing of the careful puzzling
of a quilt.

        Yet one day,
an attentive hand
        will stitch into a bed covering
vibrant masks
from these strange,
discomfiting days.

JULENE TRIPP WEAVER

PLEASE REMEMBER

I was an herbalist
I harvested and ate wild foods daily,
drank raw milk, sought plants
to heal, made medicines, wrote
articles to educate while integrating
the wise woman tradition into my own life.

I made life happen in my kitchen:
fermentation, the most glorious soups,
shrubs, oxymels, kombucha, phases
I went through, and smoothies ever
lasting, tea brewing on the stove
so many herbs from different cultures.
No borders barred.

I wanted to change relationships through
honesty, to create an open field
without restriction, my view not the majority
I lived a different life, not marrying, not
having children, I went from the assumption
I would have children to the firm
decision I would not, it lasted a lifetime.

Open to polyamory, to having lovers
I kept my commitments, my promises.
I have no regrets, it was not a selfish
life, I gave at the office to hundreds of clients
people who remember me. I lived
a stoic life spreading goodwill, engaging
politically, doing my best for liberal
causes: to stop war, advance women,
workers, and all underclasses, I wanted

the rich to pay taxes, the stomping
down on the poor to stop, I wanted
the free flow of money, I spent my cash,
saved only enough to feel secure
in a world that is a minefield.

Collecting fennel, I thank the mother plant
leave her to nurture her sisters, watch the bees
collecting nectar, there is enough for
everyone. We live in bounty if we give and take
with love, not hoard or covet from one another.
There is an open kitchen in my heart
a way to peace in this world. Peace is a verb
if we make it so. Turn war to a noun and let
it sit, this my heart speaks. Remember
I signed many petitions daily to save
the world we exist within; the planet will
continue when we stop, but any damage
is too much. We are the only people
who can save us and we're way out of line.
Our roadblocks our biggest lesson
I found my way through many.
Know my friendliness, my kind heart that
opens to little children and animals.
Know my soul is an icebreaker as arctic
sheets of ice crash down, their screams
echo through chambered hearts, the ache
of our planet I know well. The planet will
remain with its small critters, its agile
roaches and rats, it is we humans who will die.
I tried in my way to steer us from the void.

KATHLEEN ROXBY

THE END CAME

There was a door
Where none belonged.
As she paused at its threshold,
Though her light was failing,
The magnificence of her sunset
Lit the sky, all the scene before us
Filling the air, the world
With the brilliance
Of her good-bye.

RHONDA SEITER

HAIKU

The lilypad rests
atop water. Buoyancy
befriends gravity.

WHAT IF

What if I became at complete peace with what is? Ah, what then... I could settle into this glorious gift of my life, no longer looking to the what ifs of the past, and not fearing the what ifs of my future. Each day would unfold gently like a flower in my hand, a bud in the morning dew, slowly opening as the day progressed and the sun traveled across the sky. What if I never forced its opening, letting it follow its natural course, never squeezing it too hard, or watering it too heavily? What if I didn't fertilize it to make it bigger, or close my hand to hide it and make it smaller? What if I didn't enter it into garden competitions longing for the blue ribbon prize of best of show? What if it was prickly like a thistle, gangly like a sunflower, or earthly pale like a mushroom just finding its place in the world? Could I be still and wait, drinking in nature's quietness and savor the what is? I long to be reborn into the now holding each precious day, creating a bright and fulfilling future in acceptance.

> What if What is
> What if is my battered boat
> What is brings me home

There was   pause

and the humans were afraid
and grasses in the meadow
were still

and hawks who loved
to hunt small creatures
circled.

Pews   barren of bodies
infected with yesterday's prayers
exhaled.

Frayed with bewilderment
hymnals released a scent of sorrow
and what had not been memorized
stayed shut.

Outside the open door   beyond
the worn stone steps
air moved.   Birds

blustery with spring lust
ransacked back lots and alleys for
sticks and dead grass.

Humans   so hidden
it was as if   cloud and root and hill
demanded

     Stay back   stay away   stay in.
     Face your smeared windows
     your unread holy texts.

     There will be re-arrangement

of angels   animals   and humankind—
order inclined toward   insect   ocean   and oak.

Reckon with and return
when you have learned
tiferet   *chesed.*

Then   open your door
curl your shoulders down
walk   as it is commanded by beast
and breeze and blue black dusk

into remnants   of holiness   and grace

(tiferet, harmony; chesed, lovingkindness)

KM BELLAVITA is a soul born of the city but most comfortable surrounded by the drama of nature, an avid traveler who is always happy to come home. KM Bellavita writes on white lined 8.5 x 11 pads with pencil—nothing is permanent.

JAYNE BENJULIAN is the author of *Five Sextillion Atoms*. Her work appears in numerous literary and performance journals and anthologies. Jayne served as chief speechwriter at Apple, investigator for the public defender in King County, Washington and director of new play development at Magic Theater in San Francisco. She was an Ossabaw Island Project Fellow; teaching fellow at Emory University; lecturer in the Graduate Program in Theater at San Francisco State University; and Fulbright Teaching Fellow in Lyon, France. Next year, she will be a resident at the Tyrone Guthrie Centre, Ireland. She earned an MA at Emory University and an MFA from the Warren Wilson Program for Writers. Her new poetry collection, out to publishers now, is *Stone in a Tree*. Jayne founded the Berkshire Writers Project, where she helps artists develop their book projects and teaches the writing and performance of poetry and monologue. She coaches speech and debate at Stoneleigh-Burnham School.

TONI (PETERSON) BIXBY was born in Minneapolis, Minnesota. At the age of thirty-three, she fled the Minnesota winters, first to Seattle, then to Santa Barbara. She began writing fiction and non-fiction in 1990 and poetry in 2001. Her poems often reflect her life circumstances and her career as a lawyer for Child Welfare Services. She retired in 2019, and like many, spent 2020 at home, stunned by the speed and destruction of the pandemic.

VALERIE ANNE BURNS will be one of the Rituals anthology contributors with her essay, "Off God," from her book, *Caution: Mermaid Crossing, Voyages of a Motherless Daughter* published by Bell Press, November 2022. Other essays published from her book include "Gulfstream Awakening" in The Remnant Archive, November 2022; "Flying Nighties" in *Chicken Soup for the Soul: Tough Times Won't Last but Tough People Will*, released November 2021. Two essays were published in *HerStry Literary Magazine*: "Venice Vision," September 2020 and "Your Bed," May 2021, among others. In September 2021, she received a Finalist Award from Page Turner Awards in the category of manuscript submission. In addition, she was sponsored by a breast cancer nonprofit retreat organization on a trip to Italy and The Dominican Republic to present her workshop, "Living and Healing Through Color." She traveled to Rome in September 2022 for the same nonprofit, where she blogged about her experience.

MATTIE COLL is a retired English instructor who authored a book of poetry, *The Journey*, and has written essays for local magazines and papers. She lives in Richmond, VA, with her black Lab, Flip.

AMANDA SUE CREASEY has been compelled to write since she could hold a pencil. A speculative fiction author whose debut novel will launch in 2023, Amanda is also a high school English teacher and the Outdoors Writer for Cooperative Living Magazine. She holds an undergraduate degree in German, English, and Secondary Education from Michigan State University and a graduate degree in Creative Writing from the University of Denver. Her work appears in three *Chicken Soup for the Soul* books, and her poetry, outdoor journalism, and photography have earned recognition from The Poetry Society of Virginia and Virginia Outdoor Writers Association. When she isn't writing, she enjoys hiking, walking, and paddleboarding with her dogs. A member of James River Writers, the Poetry Society of Virginia, and Virginia Outdoor Writers Association, she resides in Virginia with her husband and two rescue dogs, Nacho and Soda, chihuahua/terrier littermates who rule the house.

AMY ELISABETH DAVIS grew up in a corner of New York City between Van Cortlandt Park and the Hudson River. She now lives in Los Angeles. A historian as well as a poet, she holds an AB from Cornell University and a Ph.D. from Columbia University. Her work has appeared in *Tar River Poetry*, *december*, *The Southern Humanities Review* (honorable mention for the Jake Adam York Prize), *The Free State Review*, *Levure littéraire*, *Crab Orchard Review*, *Spillway*, *Women's Studies*, and elsewhere. She is the co-editor of *Written Here: The Community of Writers Poetry Review 2016* and was the recipient of a month-long writing residency at Yefe Nof in autumn 2018.

MELISSA FACE is the author of the award-winning collection *I Love You More Than Coffee: Essays on*

Parenthood and *I Love You More Than Coffee: A Guided Journal for Moms* (September 13, 2022). Her writing has appeared in numerous local and national publications, including *Richmond Family Magazine*, *Charlottesville Family Magazine*, *Tidewater Family Magazine*, *Scary Mommy*, *Motherscope*, *Guideposts*, *Nine Lives: A Life in Ten Minutes Anthology*, *Parhelion Literary Magazine*, and twenty-six volumes of *Chicken Soup for the Soul*.

NINA GABY is a writer, visual artist and psychiatric nurse practitioner who spent the pandemic hunkered down across from the longest floating bridge east of the Mississippi, maintaining a clinical practice from her kitchen counter while trying to finish a memoir. The last chapter of the memoir is writing itself as Gaby moves on to new digs in an arty neighborhood in her upstate New York hometown. Gaby's essays and articles have been published in numerous anthologies, journals and magazines and she is the editor of *"Dumped: Stories of Women Unfriending Women."* Her artwork is held in various collections, including the Smithsonian, Arizona State University and Rochester Institute of Technology. More at www.ninagaby.com.

GRETCHEN GALES is a content writer by day, and executive editor of *Quail Bell Magazine* by night. Her work has been published in *Bustle*, *Next Avenue*, *The Huffington Post*, *YourTango*, and others. See more of Gretchen's work at www.writinggales.com.

JOHN GLANVILLE has been writing for a little less than sixty-five years, long enough to have developed a unique style of conversational prose and short enough to think he has more to say. John has enjoyed his time with the Writing Through the Apocalypse writers group and appreciates all Marcia Meier brings to the task of herding this special group of cats. John looks forward to seeing our writing in print, in order to reflect and remember on the time, not long ago, when we were locked in with no place to go, except Saturday mornings with our writer friends.

Raised on a family farm in northwestern Missouri, JULIANA LIGHTLE became a singer, college administrator, corporate manager and consultant, racehorse breeder, educator, and author. She holds a Ph.D. in counseling from The Ohio State University, B.A. in English from URI, as well as other degrees. Her three published books include one on sexual harassment prevention, co-authored with an attorney; a memoir in poetry; and most recently *You're Gonna Eat That!? Adventures with Food, Family, and Friends.* After spending many years in the Panhandle of Texas, she recently moved to Southern California, where she continues to work with high school students, write, garden, and sing.

JOAN MAZZA worked as a medical microbiologist, psychotherapist, and taught workshops on understanding dreams and nightmares. She is the author of six self-help psychology books, including *Dreaming Your Real Self.* Her poetry has appeared in *The Comstock Review, Prairie Schooner, Slant, Poet Lore,* and *The Nation.* She lives in rural central Virginia and writes every day.

MARCIA MEIER'S memoir, *Face,* published in 2021 by Saddle Road Press, won numerous awards, including the New Mexico-Arizona Book Award. She has been a professional journalist and writer for many years, and in 2021 began a teaching career trying to teach English language arts to middle-schoolers. She's still trying.

GOLNAZ MONTAGNÉ is a retired civil engineer, management coach, and writer who has lived in downtown Marseille, France, since 2018. She was born in Iran and lived there until the end of high school. She has lived in France since 1974. She also lived for fifteen years in three different states in the United States. She is now a caregiver to her college sweetheart-husband of twenty-six years, who is a bedridden retired engineer and a polio survivor. Golnaz enjoyed the excitement and quietness caused by the different lockdowns imposed by the French government during the Covid-19 pandemic. She felt that she was finally part of the community, as everyone else was in home jail like her. Birds, silence and wild nature also found their way back to urban Marseille around her.

SHAUNA POTOCKY is a writer, poet and painter who calls Seward, Alaska, home. Shauna has a deep love of high peaks, jagged ridgelines and ice. She has a strong connection to the natural world—including both landscapes and seascapes with their rough or subtle edges where life unfolds. Shauna is the author of *Yosemite Dawning, Poems of the Sierra Nevada*, published by Cirque Press. Shauna's work has appeared in publications such as *Alaska Women Speak, Beyond Words International Literary Journal, Cirque Journal*, and The *Seward Sun*.

TANIA PRYPUTNIEWICZ is the author of the full-length poetry collection *November Butterfly* (Saddle Road Press, 2014), *Heart's Compass Tarot: Discover Tarot Journaling and Create Your Own Cards* (Two Fine Crows Books, 2021), and a memoir-in-poems, *The Fool in the Corn* (Saddle Road Press, 2022). A graduate of the Iowa Writers' Workshop, Tania lives in Coronado and teaches poetry and tarot-inspired writing classes for San Diego Writers, Ink and Antioch University's Continuing Education program. She lives in Coronado with her husband, three children, their Siberian husky and formerly feral feline named Luna.

LISA RIZZO is the author of *Always a Blue House* (Saddle Road Press, 2016), finalist in the 2016 National Federation of Press Woman Awards, and *In the Poem an Ocean* (Big Table Publishing, 2011). Her work appears in journals and anthologies including *Longridge Review, The MacGuffin, Rain Taxi, Brevity Blog,* and *Unmasked, Women Over Fifty Write About Sex and Intimacy* (Weeping Willow Books). One of her essays was a finalist in the 2019 Willamette Writers Kay Snow Awards. She is a 2022 writer-in-residence at Craigardan Collective. You can visit her in Portland, Oregon, or at www. lisarizzowriter.com.

BARBARA ROCKMAN is author of *Sting and Nest,* winner of the New Mexico-Arizona Book Award and *to cleave,* winner of the National Press Women Poetry Prize and finalist for the International Book Award. Her poems have appeared in *Calyx, Thrush,* terrain.org, *Bellingham Review, Southern Humanities Review,* and *Nimrod.* Barbara teaches poetry at Esperanza Shelter for Battered Families, in community workshops and at Santa Fe Community College. She coordinates the Poets@HERE Gallery reading series in Santa Fe and is a frequent image and word collaborator with artists. Barbara holds an MFA in writing from Vermont College of Fine Arts.

KATHLEEN ROXBY is a prize-winning poet with work published in anthologies, poetry magazines and three chapbooks. She has been a poetry judge, facilitator of two poetry groups, editor of a poetry magazine, anthology, and chapbooks for her mother and her two anthologies, also one for her father. Her favorite poets are Poe, Issa and Li Po Chu'i, with a special place for Benet's "John Brown's Body." Her prose appeared on a website dedicated to writing. Kathleen had several day jobs: clerk, teacher, secretary, and computer system administrator. Kathleen's interests include theater, dancing, painting and reading. She is a native of California and resides in Santa Barbara with her dog, Opal.

RHONDA JEAN SEITER, a former high school art teacher, believes creativity in all its forms is spiritual and accessible to everyone. She currently writes screenplays.

Since childhood, NANCY A. SHOBE has had an insatiable curiosity about the human experience and what lies beyond. She began her writing career in Chicago and was eventually "blown west" to Santa Barbara where she wrote the travel book *The Insiders' Guide to Santa Barbara*, the documentary film *Above Santa Barbara*, travel guides for conference/visitors bureaus, and articles for news portals. Her essays and short stories have appeared in *The Penman Review*, *The Storyteller Anthology*, *The Helix Literary Magazine*, and *Shark Reef Journal*. Nancy performed her story *Death by Design* to two sold-out audiences and is now a certified spiritual medium.

PATRICIA SMITH is the author of *The Year of Needy Girls*, a Lambda Literary Award finalist. She received her MFA from Virginia Commonwealth University. Her fiction has appeared in such places as *Blue Mountain Review*, *Master's Review*, *So to Speak*, and *The Tusculum Review*. Her nonfiction has appeared most recently in *Feels Blind Literary*, where it was nominated for a Pushcart. Other publications include *Hippocampus*, *Broad Street: A New Magazine of True Stories*, *Parhelion Literary Magazine*, *Prime Number*, and *Gris Gris* as well as in several anthologies. Additionally, her work was chosen to be highlighted in *From Page to Stage*, choreographed and performed by Starr Foster Dance Co. in Richmond, VA. A native New Englander, she lives with her wife in Chester, VA, and teaches American literature and creative writing at the Appomattox Regional Governor's School in Petersburg, VA.

LAURNA STRIKWERDA is a freelance writer in Ottawa, Ontario, who writes on parenting, faith, art, and activism. Her writing has appeared in *Sojourners*, *US Catholic*, *Waging Nonviolence*, and *The Christian Century*.

After graduating from UCSB, JUSTINE SUTTON adopted Santa Barbara as her hometown. Since her internship at the SB Independent in 1991, she has covered arts for local media outlets, writing countless reviews of theater and dance performances. After some time in the Bay Area, where she studied belly dance and burlesque among other artistic pursuits, Justine returned to her beloved seaside town in 2005. In recent years, she has performed spoken word poetry with the ANIMA and NECTAR collectives and has dabbled in improv, storytelling, and stand-up comedy. In 2020 she began training as a voice actor and became a certified Life-Cycle® Celebrant, performing customized weddings, funerals, and ceremonies for all important moments in life. Justine writes fiction and memoir and is working on her first novel.

ANDREA VAN DER HOEK is a pediatric emergency nurse working in public health. She is passionate about reforming health care systems, increasing support for mental health, mothering, and animals. She is a member of Mary Adkins' writing program, the Book Incubator. She can't resist a sweet treat, a catchy ad jingle, or a good dad joke. Andrea lives in the Midwest with her family, two dogs, and guinea pig.

CLAIRE VAN BLARICUM, a resident of Santa Barbara, California, has worked as a high school science teacher, Natural History Museum docent, administrator for a local senior citizen charity, Civil Service Commissioner, and member of the Santa Barbara School Board. She has always been an advocate for libraries, attending the 1991 White House Conference on Libraries as a California delegate, and serving for many years on the Santa Barbara County Library Advisory Committee. She has served on the boards of several non-profit organizations, including the Santa Barbara Education Foundation, Postpartum Support International, and Women to Women International. Claire is currently on the board of the League of Women Voters of Santa Barbara. She often moderates candidate and issue forums for the league. Claire has been a member of the local American Association of University Women branch since 1972, serving in a number of capacities over the years, including president. She currently participates in the AAUW branch Writing Group.

ALENKA VRECEK was born at the foot of the Alps in Slovenia, a part of former communist Yugoslavia. Born with a spirit for adventure, she came to America at twenty years old with a backpack, a pair of skis, and a pocket full of dreams. She was a ski coach and a director of pedagogy for Squaw Valley and Alpine Meadows Ski Teams for thirty years. Alenka owns Tahoe Tea Company and lives in Lake Tahoe, California, with her second husband, Jim, their four children, three grandchildren, and a golden retriever named Monty. Her debut memoir, *She Rides, Chasing Dreams through California and Mexico*, will be published on June 13, 2023.

JAMIE WALLACE believes in daily chocolate, small kindnesses, and the magic of stories. She began journaling at age seven, read *The Lord of the Rings* for the first time in third grade, and has never stopped looking for magic in both the everyday world and the books she reads. Though she is, by most standards, a "woman of a certain age," she is still trying to figure out what she wants to be when she grows up. She hopes to one day find her way to sharing some of her stories and other enchantments with people outside her own head. For now, she continues to write, read, pat every dog she meets, talk to crows, and ride horses. Find her on Instagram as @suddenlyjamie.

JULENE TRIPP WEAVER is a psychotherapist and writer in Seattle, WA. Her third poetry collection, *truth be bold– Serenading Life & Death in the Age of AIDS*, was a finalist for the Lambda Literary Awards and won the Bisexual Book Award. Recent publications include: *HEAL, Autumn Sky Poetry, Poetry Super Highway, As it Ought To Be, Feels Blind*, and the anthology *Poets Speaking to Poets: Echoes and Tributes*. More of her writing can be found at www.julenetrippweaver.com, or though Linktree linktr.ee/julenetweaver.

KATHRYN WOOD is a woman in love with all things unhinged. She lives in Richmond, Virginia, though she longs hourly for the narrow cobblestone streets of Rome and Naples. Foremost she is a wanderer, a maker, a dancer, a shower singer. She graduated from University of Virginia in 2018 with degrees in English and Women, Gender & Sexuality and from Virginia Commonwealth University in 2021 with a bachelor of science in nursing. She has just begun a career working as a nurse in the Neonatal Intensive Care Unit in Richmond and hopes in her free-time to behave more badly than her uniformed position allows. Her poem *Ragdolls* can be found in Boston College's Undergraduate Feminist Anthology, *Hoochie* (2017). She is currently editing her first book.

Deborah Alston Wroblewski is a wife, mother, and grandmother living in Santa Barbara, California. She is a former nurse and art teacher, who has always viewed writing as a tool for healing. Her work has formally been published in The Sun and in Somerset Studios magazine. She is honored to be part of this anthology.

George Yatchisin is the author of *Feast Days* (Flutter Press 2016) and *The First Night We Thought the World Would End* (Brandenburg Press 2019). His poems have been published in journals including *Antioch Review*, *Askew*, and *Zocalo Public Square*. He is co-editor of the anthology *Rare Feathers: Poems on Birds & Art* (Gunpowder Press 2015), and his poetry appears in anthologies including *Reel Verse: Poems About the Movies* (Everyman's Library 2019).

CPSIA information can be obtained
at www.ICGtesting.com
Printed in the USA
JSHW050335270223
38242JS00006B/17